Y0-CLH-951

And We Have Danced

cover photos: (front cover) Gregory Mitchell dancing Psalm 8 at 1977 Sacred Dance Guild Closing Worship during June Institute.

(back cover) Forrest Coggan leading the people in congregational dancing at Michigan Sacred Dance Guild Worship.

The following members of the Sacred Dance Guild were voted honorary life members through the past twenty years because of their contributions to Sacred Dance and the shaping of the Sacred Dance Guild:

Ruth St. Denis
Ted Shawn
Jess Meeker
Mary Anthony
Forrest Coggan
Matteo
Arthur Hall
Betty Ford

AND WE HAVE DANCED

A History of the Sacred Dance Guild

1958 - 1978

by

Carlynn Reed

edited by Doug Adams

THE SHARING COMPANY

 For information, inquire from The Sharing Company, P. O. Box 2224, Austin, Texas 78767. Additonal copies of this book are available at $5.95 per paperback copy.

Dedicated in loving memory of
Virginia Lucke
who initially asked me to write the history of the Sacred Dance Guild and whose beautiful dancing spirit was an inspiration to all who knew her.

ACKNOWLEDGEMENTS

I am deeply grateful to all those who have helped and supported me through the writing of this history. Among them I would like to express my gratitude to the following. Thanks first to Doug Adams who has encouraged me during all the stages of research and writing. He believed in me and I was strengthened by his positive energy. My deepest appreciation also goes to Mary Jane Wolbers who, in spite of extreme illness in her family, managed to read the manuscript and give very helpful suggestions. And to my husband, David, who understood the papers covering the dining room table for months, who patiently acted as a sounding board for my ideas, who gently helped to reword an awkward sentence -- my gratitude, my respect, and my love.

Carlynn L. Reed

AND WE HAVE DANCED:

A History of the Sacred Dance Guild

Chapter Titles:

INTRODUCTION

CHAPTER I " . . . to stimulate interest in dance as a religious art form . . ." (1958 - 1962)

CHAPTER II " . . . an effort to bring some order . . ." (1962 - 1965)

CHAPTER III " . . . may be the last year the Sacred Dance Guild exists as we know it . . ." (1966 - 1968)

CHAPTER IV " . . . a dream that needs to pick up steam . . ." (1968 - 1974)

CHAPTER V " . . . building a floor under sacred dance . . ." (1975 - 1978)

CHAPTER VI " . . . seven main streams in Sacred Dance . . ." (1958 - 1978)

EPILOGUE " . . . moving from the axial to the locomotor . . ." (The Twentieth Anniversary S. D. G. Festival)

APPENDICES

I: By-Laws in 1978

APPENDICES cont.

II: S. D. G. Proposed Organizational Chart (1968)

III: Officers Of the S. D. G. 1958 - 1978.

IV: Annual Workshop Leaders 1958 - 1978.

V: S. D. G. Membership Statistics 1958 - 1978.

VI: Membership By State and Country 1963 - 1978.

VII: Sacred Dance Degree Programs at Pacific School of Religion. Berkeley, California M. Div., M. A., Ph. D.

VIII: Photo History of the Sacred Dance Guild.

IX: Photo Essay of June Institute 1977.

X: Photo Essay of June Institute 1978.

BIBLIOGRAPHY

INTRODUCTION

The story of the Sacred Dance Guild officially began twenty years ago, in 1958; but, as with any organized endeavor, the events giving rise to its inception have their own importance. Dancing in the sanctuary certainly did not begin in the 1950's. Indeed, in varying degrees, dance has always existed in the Church and in virtually all religious faiths. The history of the Western Church has reflected a variety of attitudes toward religious dance; and the twentieth century has chosen to regard it with increasing favor. With the aid of 1) the rise of modern dance and 2) a more open response on the part of church leaders, dancers who wanted to express their faith through movement have found the tools in the new technique and the place in many sanctuaries.

By 1956 there was enough activity in New England that the Eastern Regional Sacred Dance Association was formed. Membership came basically from directors of sacred dance choirs who wanted to share and to learn. Many, if not most, were untrained dancers who wished to express their worship through movement. In 1957, a Newsletter was begun which was intended for collection into a handbook of ideas and guidelines. It included stick figure choreography, hints on robing, lighting, Scriptural texts, music, bibliography, and teaching techniques. In May, Jane Renz of Pennsylvania wrote the first article called "Dance in Church" which encouraged members to balance religious integrity with dance ability. She said the message must take precedence over the dance, but the dance should be done well.

The succeeding issues gave specific suggestions on robing (use modesty and "common sense"), lighting, etc., but encouraged the scattered dance choirs to discover their own dance identity. Jean Miller of New York wrote in an article entitled, "Why Have A Religious Dance Choir?", that dancers should not attempt gestures that were too difficult for them. It would be better, she said, to begin realistically by offering a simpler movement and work toward the level of proficiency required to dance the more demanding combinations.

In a letter recorded in the Newsletter in late 1957, Mary Jane Wolbers expressed concern over the frantic search by many dance choirs for stick figure choreography. She felt that this unhealty dependence upon a few professionals would hamper the growth of sacred dance. As a solution, Mary Jane suggested that the Eastern Regional Sacred Dance Association provide workshops which would teach the basics of creative movement so that dance choirs could learn to solve their own choreographic problems. Mary Jane's foresight has enabled local dance choirs to develop their own identity as their individual creativity took root.

In that same *Newsletter*, entitled "Don't You Agree", Jane Renz, editor, expressed her opinion as to the main purpose of the Association, i.e., to give the church leader more dance knowledge and the dancer more religious training. She felt that the Association should be a balancing center between the two ingredients of "sacred" and "dance". The reader would do well to keep Jane's thoughts in mind throughout the ensuing history.

The time limits of this history are the years from 1958 to 1978. I have chosen not to go into detail on the years preceding the inception of the Sacred Dance Guild. The history follows three basic threads which interweave to reflect the development of the Guild's identity. The first is the organizational machinery which has attempted to lead and guide the Guild. The second is thoughtful essays written on the subject of sacred dance, by both members and non-members. The third is the variety of dance activities in which the members have engaged over the years. My primary sources are the *Newsletter* edited three times a year, the minutes of meetings, and personal correspondence. This history attempts to portray the life of the Guild through its many members. Although a few people stand out because of their contribution in leadership positions, this history is not a series of biographies of significant personalities. Rather, greater attention is given to the activities and thoughts reported to the *Newsletter* which appear to indicate particular trends within the Guild.

In the final chapter, the reader is given a brief description of the Sacred Dance Guild of 1978 -- the many directions of sacred dance which are borne out of the previous twenty years. I have attempted to interpret the raw data of the primary sources into significant stages of historical development. Although I am a member of the Guild, I have tried to be objective enough to reveal the weaknesses as well as the strengths. There is much to criticize in the Guild and much to commend.

The importance of this history rests in two complementary contributions. First, it is the official history of the Sacred Dance Guild, and thus has personal value to everyone who has been a member. And second, the Guild itself is an important force in the world of religion today as it raises questions about the relationship of the spirit of the person with the movement of the body, and more deeply, the relationship of the whole person with God, and people with one another. This history is the story of a people who have hearkened to the Divine Piper and have danced.

CHAPTER I

1958-1962

On February 10, 1958, several people who had been active in sacred dance and had already been members in the Eastern Regional Sacred Dance Association, met at their annual meeting in Winchester, Massachusetts and, having realized the geographical restriction of their name, voted to henceforth be called the SACRED DANCE GUILD. Even at this time there were a few members in Texas, Illinois, Colorado, and California which made the Eastern designation unrealistic and unworkable. The original organization was only two years old, but much planning and discussion on needed changes and direction had obviously preceded this date. New by-laws had been drawn up and, except for a few alterations, were voted on in the meeting. (See Appendix I) The slate of officers was presented,and Jane Renz became the first President of the Sacred Dance Guild.

The original purpose of the Guild, as stated in Article II of the By-Laws was "to stimulate interest in dance as a religious art form, and to provide a means of communication and training for dance choirs." To achieve this end, the activities directly sponsored by the Guild included: 1) a two-day February workshop with annual meeting, 2) a one-day Spring Festival usually sometime in May, 3) a three-day workshop in June, 4) a one-day workshop in the Fall, and 5) a Newsletter distributed in the Spring, Fall, and Winter of each year. This was an extremely ambitious yearly program, and these activities, which basically contain the historical development of the Guild, took the attention, time, and energy of the leaders of the organization. Each one of these five items required someone who knew how to organize, was willing to work very hard, and was sensitive to the needs of the sacred dance members.

The Newsletter has been the life-line of the Guild since the very first issue. It contained reports of past events, information on coming events, reading suggestions, list of membership activities, and articles by people within and outside the Guild. Some of these articles give us a great deal of insight into the early concerns of the leadership. For example, in May, 1958, the purposes of a motion choir were described:

. . .to unite teenage girls in a religious

> atmosphere for experience of togetherness and belonging -- to each other and to that Infinite Beauty and Wisdom outside of themselves, . . . to develop an awareness of themselves, their potentialities, . . . to provide a medium and atmosphere for exploring: the use and meaning of their bodies . . ., their creative imagination . . ., their spirits . . ., interpersonal relationships, . . . to discover the joy of service, . . . to provide a wealth of experience and knowledge for mature adulthood. (Newsletter, May, 1958, p. 1.)

On basically the same theme, in the September, 1959 <u>Newsletter</u>, President Jane Renz wrote an article to answer the question: Why have a dance choir? She said there was benefit to the choir members themselves both in religious understanding and emotional outlet, not to mention the physical benefits to the body in strength and grace. The congregation was benefitted by the communication of the message, which was aided by the sincerity and dedication of the choir. Thus, in keeping with the purpose of the Sacred Dance Guild, both the <u>Newsletter</u> and the many workshops emphasized the needs of the rhythmic choir. Teaching was always available on the purpose of a sacred dance choir, how to get started, standards to be aimed for, etc. (Minutes, June, 1961.)
And with the help of the ideas from Newsletters, workshops, and individual members, as well as

sheer spontaneity, rhythmic choirs gradually began springing up all over the county. This, of course, was the hope of the Guild, and early growth followed a healthy pattern.

As sacred dance activity became more and more widespread,evaluation and self-reflection followed closely. In trying to understand who they were and what they were doing, some members attempted to gather the movement of sacred dance into a working vocabulary. As early as June, 1961, it was suggested in an executive meeting that an iconography or language of sacred dance be developed. However, it was vetoed for reasons that have been lost. We can only guess that perhaps the leaders felt that either the organization was too young and setting rigid definitions would be premature, or that a specialized art form like sacred dance could not be reduced to a glossary of terms. Whatever the reason, it was not an acceptable suggestion at the time; and it never come up again as an issue.

Yet, the need to capture in words some of the essence of sacred dance persisted; and we can see in almost every Newsletter contributions to the thought and philosophy of dance, especially as it pertained to religious experience. And so, along with the concerns for helping dancers start rhythmic choirs, the leadership recognized the need for intelligent statements on the area of sacred dance from theologians, philosophers, and artists, members and non-members alike. For example, Paul Tillich, professor at Harvard Divinity School and noted theologian, was quoted at length in the <u>News-letter</u> of May, 1958. In answer to the question "The Dance: What It Means To Me," Professor Tillich reflected on the relationship between religion and culture, and the problem of the Protestant (because of a basic depreciation of the body) criticizing dance as evil. Puritanism, said Tillich, had cut the "primordial tie between religion and dance." (<u>Newsletter</u>, May, 1958, p. 2.) Moshe Davis, Professor and Director of the Jewish Theological Seminary of America, was quoted at the same time, in answer to the same question:

> I dance at least three times a day -- at morning, afternoon and evening prayers. I was brought up in a mode of worship in which movement is a part of the act of prayer, and I find that I pray with greater intensity when my prayer is accompanied by an informal rhythmic pattern. Dance, to me, is not essentially a performance to watch, but a form of personal expression. . . Jewish religious leaders and educators in America are keenly aware of the role of dance education in unfolding the personality and helping the individual to discover his

> relationship to God and the world he lives in . . . (Unfortunately) individualized chanting in prayers has been sublimated into uniform congregational singing and personalized movement has been inhibited by the demand of group decorum and 'solidity'. Happily, the movement to make the dance a basic part of the Jewish educational scheme is gaining. . .. I look forward to the day when it will be part of the curriculum of life to learn how to take the long step back into ourselves, so that we will feel free to dance as we feel free to walk. (Newsletter, May, 1958, p. 2.)

I have quoted from Dr. Davis at some length to show the thoughts of a theologically astute person outside of the Sacred Dance Guild who had a profound understanding of the human person and the nature of dance. His description of the naturalness of dance in prayer and the unnaturalness of conforming to a non-moving uncreative sameness with the "group" for the sake of "decorum and solidity" is prophetic of what is slowly happening in the mid to late 1970's. Many of the points Dr. Davis discussed have been rehearsed and elaborated upon through the years in the Newsletters of the Sacred Dance Guild.

Reminiscent of Dr. Davis' rejection of homogeneity, members of the Guild were soon reflecting several different streams of thought. Articles and letters to the editor were submitted to explain what sacred dancers do and why they do it -- to evaluate, criticize, and raise questions -- even to disagree. Guild members, committed to a common purpose, and all dancers in worship discovered very early in their history their heterogeneous nature. For a few this was somewhat upsetting. But as Editor Mrs. Norman Saunders so gently admonished in her editorial of the September, 1960 Newsletter:

> There will necessarily be some conflicting ideas. This is good, healthy, normal and democratic. You must creatively choose those which you feel fit your Church and and your own peculiar situations. (Newsletter, September, 1960, p. 1.)

So, breadth, or at least the attempt at breadth, existed from the outset, and as the reader will discover, this breadth of sharing grew over the years until today the Newsletter reflects beautifully the wide scope of religious dance in America and around the world.

Among the writers of wisdom in the area of sacred dance, Margaret Taylor must take a leading place. Perhaps more than any other person, Margaret has influenced the development of sacred dance in America. She is quoted in the June 1961 Newsletter:

> The art of symbolic movement is alive with the whole being involved. At times it communicates beauty and meaningfulness; at times it stabs us into a new awareness of agony and distortion; at times it reveals the resilience of souls in the midst of confusion, yet relating to ultimate concerns.
> The basic requisite of this art is that the participants and leaders are clearly dedicated to use their whole being (body,

mind, soul) with integrity as they confront present day issues which become clarified and illumined as the outgrowth of their deepening understanding.
Sacred Dance has the primary responsibility to be 'sacred' and that means (by definition) that the participants are 'dedicated and set apart in honor of God.' It means that each participant is disciplined spiritually, sensitively aware of others' needs, and undergirded by a vital sense of the power and the presence of God. This 'sacred' quality is communicated to others; its absence is obvious.
The secondary responsibility of sacred dance is 'dance'. The movements should grow creatively out of inner motivation, not geared to any specific dance style nor self-consciously involved in body techniques. The dance movements and designs are secondary to the sacred concerns that are being communicated, allowing the clear revelation of the spirit through the body disciplined for this purpose and diffused with the spirit. (Newsletter, June, 1961, p. 5.)

Again, I have quoted at great length for two reasons: 1) to show that intelligent, reflective statements were shared through the Newsletters at a very early date, and 2) to reveal the concerns of the early period as those which remain with the Guild today. First, Margaret said that dance comes through the whole being, not just the body. This concept of the unity of the whole person in movement is increasingly understood today, especially in the light of developments in the area of Dance Therapy.* Then, Margaret told of the breadth of the intentions of sacred dance. The choreographer must be sensitive to contemporary issues in creating dances and be somewhat of a prophet in dealing with "today". It is encumbent that the true experiences of the soul, the agony as well as the beauty, be unveiled. Too often, Margaret said, only the lovely and beautiful, have been shown. Integrity demands that full truth be revealed.

Margaret then discussed carefully the relationship between 'sacred' and 'dance'. Her position is very clear: the 'sacred' is the dancer's primary responsibility. It is important to take note, not only of Margaret's stand on this issue, but also the very fact of

---

* Throughout this book, there are many references to dance therapy. I would like to acknowledge the American Dance Therapy Association whose standards are highly professional. There are many members of the Guild whose interest and qualifications are not on the level of a registered Dance Therapist, but who are concerned at a lay level with helping others to wholeness through dance. I will capitalize "Dance Therapy" when used professionally, and will use lower case letters when used nonprofessionally.

the discussion. The whole debate on the relative importance of 'sacred' and 'dance' has occupied much of the thought and concern of the Guild throughout its entire history. Many articles would be written, some criticizing the lack of apparent spiritual direction, some lamenting the lack of fundamental dance training.

In January of 1962, Leda Canino, leader at several sacred dance workshops, wrote an article which laid bare a deep criticism of sacred dance choirs. Credit must go to the Guild for allowing and even encouraging the kind of unfavorable evaluation that Leda gave:

> At various motion choir presentations I have become troubled at the lack of truly powerful movement. True, we are to be involved a great deal in meditation, but too often our dance attempts lose their value. The energetic reaction to purpose becomes weak and too much two-dimensional posturing takes place. (Newsletter, Jan. 1962, p. 4)

These thoughts, taken from an article called, "Dancer: Revealer of Spiritual Truths", attempted to tell sacred dancers that no matter how spiritual they felt inside, the vehicle of communication, namely, the movement, had to be powerful and totally energetic. If one is to be a "revealer", then one must "reveal" -- let it be shown -- let the movement allow the spiritual truths to be unveiled. Ms. Canino suggested that weak gestures served only to bottle up and hide the spiritual.

In the same issue, comments from Sister Jean of the Episcopal Order of the Teachers of Children of God at Tuller School on Long Island, who had led a workshop at New Paltz, New York, were quoted. She, too, was obviously concerned over the lack of truly good dance among sacred dancers:

> When we offer our dance to God we must offer Him something good -- a good dance. A religious or sacred dance should be at least as good as a secular dance. Since it is inspired by God, it should be better! The dancers participating should be as good as secular dancers, both in technique and expression. We certainly owe as much to the One God as to the god of entertainment. Good technique is not an end so high it is unachievable. Dance and drama both take perspiration and inspiration. Worthwhile sentiment becomes mere sentimentality unless it is backed up with hard intelligent work. (Newsletter, Jan. 1962, p. 12.)

We can surmise from these two fairly strong statements independently offered by two respected workshop leaders that much of what they had seen was powerless and unpolished. It seems that a number of choirs were making their debut with all the enthusiasm of dancers but with little of the training. The question remained: did the spiritual dedication of the rhythmic choir make up for that lack? Obviously, there were at least a few who felt very strongly that indeed it did not.

But the need for high quality in dance was not the only element which some felt was lacking. There was also concern for the spiritual dimension. As in all of the religious arts, the "soul" of sacred dance was easily lost or at least blurred in the excitement of sharing ideas and dance experiences. The Reverend Robert Storer, for whom this remained an important issue, reflected on the workshop of February, 1960 in which there was a worship service of dance and reading. The Reverend Storer commented, "We must have more of this kind of spiritual experience at our gatherings." (<u>Newsletter</u>, April 1960, p. 1.) His statement was simple but it very profoundly revealed two things: 1) that this indeed was a spiritual experience, and 2) it stood apart from the usual. He reflected a deep yearning for that very special kind of community and fellowship that only believers can have when they come together. Mr. Storer also seems to have recognized that the very life of the Guild depended on it. What a hollow, superficial organization the Guild would have become if it had not nurtured its collective relationship with and experience of God.

Interestingly enough, in the same Newsletter, there was an article that, although the writer could not possibly have known in advance of Mr. Storer's concerned statements, revealed the "soul" in one of her dance experiences. Patricia Lawrence Jewitt described in the "Guest Column" a very special moment for her and her group of dancers. She had given an assignment and was watching the group when:

> Suddenly there was such a sense of Presence in the room . . . that each was making intimate contact. I was an intruder in God's business, and I had no right to look at His relationship with these people at this revealing moment. I had to turn away . . . with the tears that often come to us in moments of revelation. (Newsletter, April 1960, p.5.)

Something so holy occurred that as the prophets of old removed their shoes when they stood before God, so Patricia removed her sight from God's "business". Patricia shared with the Guild the very essence of sacred dance -- that it should be a clear vehicle for welcoming the Presence of God.

Thus, we see a balance of concern in the Guild. The dance performance should be stunningly excellent and powerful. And the anticipation of the Presence of God should be high. In the next chapter, two classic illustrations from both sides of this discussion will be fully presented.

A very short word should be inserted here on early glimmerings of an attempt to stretch our understanding of sacred dance. In September of 1960, Mabel Hart, director of a sacred dance choir from Montana, wrote a letter to the Newsletter saying that she had three doctors on the staff of the medical school of the University of Oregon confirm her feelings "that Rhythmic Choir/Sacred Dance reaches and releases untouched depths of personality." (Newsletter, Sept. 1960, p. 2.) She valued Sacred Dance both as art form and as a communicator of theological truth, but it was the "therapeutic" side that excited her most. She said, "I have seen young people and older ones grow calmer, happier, wiser and more beautiful." (Ibid.) And so, dance therapy was introduced to the Guild as a valid element in the area of sacred dance. In the same issue, a little note from a member asked, "If anyone has info about work being done with retarded children in the field of Religious Dance, please write to Dr. Oliver Gordon, Department of Education, Philadelphia Council of Churches." (Newsletter, Sept. 1960, p. 5.) This was the beginning of an increasing number of reports on working with retarded children. Many Guild members became seriously involved in this field with very beautiful rewards.

The reader can see that, indeed, the Sacred Dance Guild, in its early modest beginnings could already boast of a bright and searching membership, aware of its need to reflect, evaluate, criticize, and to grow in breadth and depth as a living community of people. Mary Jane Wolbers, in 1960, offered a bibliography of Sacred Dance Source materials. Since 1958, there were always reading suggestions and book reviews to inform the membership and hopefully educate them in sacred dance and in the thinking of related arts, philosophy, and psychology. Also, in 1960 a Packet, today called the "Helps and Guidelines Kit", was begun to help new members in getting a motion choir started and giving them ideas and music resources to consider. The Newsletter, of course, was quickly recognized as that vital link with all members. Again and again, the need for communication and true sharing was encouraged by the leadership.

It would be helpful at this point to take a look at the organizational machinery which kept this flurry of activity and thought running. Of course the mere changing of the name from Eastern Regional Sacred Dance Association to Sacred Dance Guild did not change the whole complexion of the organization immediately. There were a few members in the western states; but by and large it was still an eastern centered guild and to a lesser extent would remain that way until recently, even though members were well distributed across the country. Except for the years 1969-1970 (Margaret Fisk Taylor -- Ohio), 1971-1975 (Maxine DeBruyn -- Michigan), and 1977-1979 (Doug Adams -- California), the principal leadership has been in the East. (See appendix III for lists of all past and present officers.) And, except for two February workshops (1968 in Michigan and 1970 in Ohio), the principal Sacred Dance Guild sponsored workshops have always been in the East. But with membership spread so well across the country (see appendix VI on geographic distribution of membership) and with the very fine and full activity in the West today, notably in Colorado, Oregon and California, the monopoly of the East is inevitably changing with two national institutes proposed for 1980 -- one in Denver, Colorado and the other at Beverly, Massachusetts.

What concerned the executive and annual membership meetings of the Sacred Dance Guild in those early years? Mainly, it was the workships, festivals, and Newsletter. But the specific signs of growing pains were evident as well. For example, as membership in areas increased, local workshops were held; and there followed the need to clarify the responsibilities of the Guild to the workshop -- notably the financial responsibility. This problem was first discussed in the October meeting of 1960; but it took two years before the official policy of the Guild appeared in the September 1962 Newsletter, basically stating that the Sacred Dance Guild "sanctioned" but did not "sponsor" local workshops, thereby precluding any financial involvement. Resources other than money were gladly shared. But the very fact of this particular problem of the early years points to the growth and the initiative at the grass roots level. In fact, it is quite amazing to see so early the emergence of organizational concepts that would become of paramount importance under the leadership of Pat Sonen 1966-1968 (see Chapter 4) and again today under Doug Adams. The larger question of the relationship of the Sacred Dance Guild with the local activity emerged out of the need for a policy regarding local workshops. Should local areas actually be organized under the over-arching machinery of the Executive Board of the Sacred Dance Guild? This question became a real one in June of 1961 when the Board meeting discussed the formation of a Sacred Dance chapter in Minneapolis! The minutes hardly reflect the importance of such a step. The records stated, "A new Sacred Dance Chapter has been started in Minneapolis." (Minutes, June 27, 1961.) That's all! But in the total history of the Guild, that statement takes on an historic value and probably prophetic importance.

The year 1961 appears to be somewhat of a watershed in the history of the Guild. Discussions on regional chapters had obviously begun. Scholarship aid for students attending workshops was suggested in the February meeting of that year. Obviously, the organization must have sensed its growth and importance to even introduce the topic of scholarships. At the same meeting the question of special rates for members at workshops was raised. Apparantly there were enough people outside the Guild being attracted to workshops to warrant the question; and there was the need to make it worthwhile to join the Guild. In fact, the best means of helping the Guild to grow in membership was the attendance at the workshops.

In the October meeting of that year, the notion of introducing the Sacred Dance Guild into the seminaries was presented. Not a great deal happened over the early years, but that vision was not lost; and today, present leader Doug Adams has made this one of his basic drives. (See appendix VII on the shape of M. A., M. Div., and Ph. D. degree programs in Sacred Dance.) But, that vision was seen as early as 1961, only three years after the birth of the Guild. The Sacred Dance Guild has dared to dream.

Thus, the initial years of the Guild were important ones of outlining its basic purpose, organizing vehicles of communication and sharing, and resourcefully following these through. The Guild was an energetic and dedicated group of people who shared the conviction of the timeliness of an organization such as this. There were growing pains, fumblings, and often slow action on getting things done. Sometimes the organization appeared too flimsy for the rapid geographical growth of the membership. But remember, all the Board members were volunteers, separated by many miles. At one time (February 1961) it was suggested the Newsletter be done professionally; but even that increasingly monumental task (the first issues were three or four pages , but today they run to forty pages) has remained voluntary (with Toni Intravaia in Illinois serving as editor from 1971 to the present.) But this group of volunteers did succeed in laying secure enough foundation stones that twenty years later a vital and alive organization still meets regularly for workshops and still receives a much enlarged Newsletter three times a year. The early leaders dared to dream and although those dreams were often frustrated and blurred, they were not lost. Indeed, it seems today that many of those dreams are being realized.

CHAPTER II

1962-1965

The period, 1962-1965, is notable for two reasons. One is the very strong and forceful leadership of Mary Jane Wolbers, a woman with a clear sense of the correct way to run an organization, and with a good working knowledge of what was happening in the dance world at large.* The second reason is contained somewhat in the first: the Sacred Dance Guild was in dire need of a leader to solidify the organization and to bring order to some apparent confusion of the past. In the meeting of February, 1964, for example, President Mary Jane reported, "The past year has been one of concentration on the records, by-laws, surveys for and of the Sacred Dance Guild in an effort to bring some order to haphazard records of the past. Mary Jane Wolbers has set up a system of permanent record books for each officer." (Minutes, February 25, 1964.) Mary Jane had her work cut out for her. She

* A fine, experienced dancer herself, Mary Jane brought to the Guild a professional attitude regarding the discipline of dance; and, because of her many contacts, she introduced many new resource people through workshops.

had a valuable sense of the history and future of the Guild as she struggled to set the organization on a clear path. Her work has had a profound influence on the Guild, not only because of the few years she was President, but also because Mary Jane is one of the few people who has actively served the Guild in one office or another since its beginning in 1958.

What needed work in the Guild? A letter from Virginia Lucke to Margaret Fisk Taylor, dated January 11, 1965 mentioned a number of problems. She referred to the February, 1964 meeting as being pretty tense with decisions of leadership on the agenda. Mary Jane was being urged to continue as President but had recently moved to Pennsylvania and needed time with her family to put down roots in a new community and begin local sacred dance activity. For some reason the Board was divided on how to resolve the problem of the vacancy. In her letter, Virginia suggested these were low years; but she had faith in the long haul.

A letter from Mary Jane to Virginia (dated August 23, 1963) confirmed some of this tension. Mary Jane lamented the lack of co-operation in getting the work done. Statements like, "To 'work away' all alone on these tasks is slow and often unsavory!" and, "Who cares enough to really work?" showed some of the inside pain behind the scenes. The organization really needed sharpening up at the top. Again, quoting from Mary Jane's letter: "I am working away on that business of 'job descriptions'." Observe that this sounded like "old" business, something that had been hanging over the Guild for some time and had blocked its smooth operation. This was five years after the original by-laws were drawn up, but the job descriptions were still not clear! Virginia was on the nominating committee at the time and Mary Jane encouraged her to:

> nominate <u>members</u> -- those who are sincerely interested in the Guild. Secondly we must find people who are willing to <u>work</u> and discharge the duties of their offices. Do you know how many of our executives are not Guild members at the present time? Do you know how few responses we receive to executive matters (those polled by mail I mean)?
> Do you know how little co-operation we get when it comes to executive meetings?

These were the words of a very discouraged, disillusioned, and over-worked president. Somehow, things had gotten out of hand. It was intolerable that some board members had actually not even kept up their membership in the Guild!

And yet, alongside the despair, there was the excitement of what the Sacred Dance Guild was really all about -- namely, sacred dance. In that very same letter, Mary Jane closed with a description of a new exciting venture known as the Sacred Dance Guild Choir for the purpose of, "sharing and building a repertoire of group works for demonstrations, future Festivals, etc." It was refreshing to see that no matter how bad things seemed to be at the structural level, that creative urge and that dedication to the purpose of the Guild remained very much alive.*

Before we deal with the creative accomplishments, we will look further into the specific areas of the organization where improvement and growth were attempted. A sense of frustration and an element of inertia

---

* A note in the September 1964 Newsletter informed the Guild of the "Chancel Dance Group" which was open to skilled dancers and met once a week. (Newsletter, Sept. 1964, p. 19.) Unfortunately, because of distances from one another, the members had to eventually abandon the project.

seemed to accompany the minutes of the meetings and some of the correspondence of this period. It was as though they were on the right track but the fuel was just not sufficient to keep the train moving at a steady pace.

The by-laws as accepted in 1958 were recognized very early as unworkable; and to this day, the leadership has been burdened with the task of clarifying and amending several of the articles. Questions arose concerning a policy on the number of years a member should be on the Board. The by-laws had stated three years, but some were staying on longer. (Minutes, February 21, 1962 -- Executive Board.) A policy regarding the Sponsoring member was discussed at the meeting in June 1962. At that time there seems to have been no distinction between "sponsor" and "group" categories for membership. And over the years, there has been considerable floundering on the distinctions on the kinds of membership. Even today, the question still arises, as at the June 1977 Institute and Annual Meeting, "Who is student? -- high school? college? graduate?" There is a lower fee for the student both for membership and for workshop fees, so the question is very important; and yet, the problem has never been quite finally resolved. As in many small organizations, matters are often tabled until the "next time".

An interesting example of the tension between that eagerness to push forward and that necessity to evaluate and pull the organization together is an item in the minutes of the February 25, 1964 annual meeting. It was "voted to authorize Judy Bennett to have a publicity flyer printed containing two pictures of Sacred Dance Guild activities, the statement of What is the Sacred Dance Guild, and list of current officers and directors. Ordered 3-5000 copies." (Minutes, February 25, 1964.) This move reflected that drive to grow and push forward by advertising and making the Guild known. However, in the minutes of a meeting in 1965 (the exact date is unclear -- probably around June), a very telling item was recorded: "Perhaps it is too early to start working on a brochure until we have a clear-cut picture of our organization." (Minutes, June 1965.) There it was in a nutshell. The crucial question was: "Who are we as an organization?' One might say that the Guild was really going through an identity crisis -- a very important stage in its history. The Guild recognized the question and began the very difficult task of answering it. But that rocess, which continues to this day, laid the oundation for the next administration under at Sonen to attempt to give the Sacred Dance uild a healthy workable identity with a ompletely new look.

And, even in the midst of the dire need or a "clear-cut picture of our organization", ith all the signs of getting completely ogged down, some important steps were taken. n 1962 one editor began taking the responsi- ility of the Newsletter for an entire year. rior to that three different editors had taken ach of the issues in a year. And, as it urned out, Margaret Fisk Taylor remained as ditor for four years from 1962-1966, and did phenomenal job. She elevated the position nd responsibility of the editor to a highly istinguished level. Her handling of the aterial and her beautifully balanced and en- ouraging editorials have become distinctive andmarks in the historical development of he Newsletter.

Another accomplishment during this period as the incorporation of the Guild in June 965 in New Hampshire. The event was hailed igorously by a hard working committee. How- ver, it did make undeniably clear the need actually recommended by the attorney) to revise the by-laws and to bring them into a realistic functioning order. A seemingly endless line of committees was begun (again) to perform this task -- a line which continues to today. (Doug Adams, President 1977-1979 hopes that 1978 will see the end of this line.) One of the anticipated benefits of incorporation, tax-exemption status, was finally realized in 1978. (Jary Yoos of Lexington, Massachusetts succeeded in seeing the Guild through the morass of red tape to that long-sought tax-exempt number.)

As is clear from the evidence, these were difficult years for the Guild at the executive and organizational level. Breakdowns in communication and co-operation plagued the efficiency of the Board and left many fine officers disillusioned and frustrated. But, in spite of setbacks and disorder the vision of what the Guild should and could be was not lost. It was just a matter of getting it there; and as Virginia Lucke said, there may be low years, but in the long haul we'll make it. In 1965, she wrote, "When I get a bit impatient or discouraged, I just look back to first meeting I attended." So, apparently even with the very justified complaints of haphazard leadership, someone felt there was ctually improvement since 1959 (when Virginia oined the Sacred Dance Guild).

Having examined a rather unhappy, although ar from hopeless, situation at the organi- ational level, we will now study some reflec- ions on the several activities sponsored.

By 1962, many workshops had been planned nd executed. It is notable that there was a incere attempt to be balanced. In the ebruary 21, 1962 Board meeting,

> there was considerable discussion of the need for a program balanced between providing increased technical dance help and help in the practical matters of conducting choir affairs and helping such a rarified atmosphere that our spiritual communication through the dance is unintelligible to our congregations. It was suggested we have a minister talk on <u>how</u> to put dance into a service. (<u>Minutes</u>, Feb. 21, 1962.)

s the board members planned workshops, there- ore, they were quite sensitive to the many inds of needs that dance choirs expressed. ance technique, the spiritual dimension, and ome of the very "nitty-gritty" practical uestions of a dance choir being part of a ervice -- all these aspects of sacred dance equired attention, and it was the responsibility of workshops to speak to these needs.

Panels were often incorporated into these early workshops with discussions led by dancers, dramatists, ministers, and theologians. Basic questions such as "What makes a dance sacred?" provided the opportunity for disciplined reflection. Many points of view were represented, and this helped many a concerned member think through his or her own position on the various discussion topics.

And, the members wanted to talk and share and explore and find out what each other was thinking and doing. Ruth Rayton, in her report of the Sacred Dance Guild Festival in the prestigious Hopkins Center at Dartmouth College in Hanover, New Hampshire in 1963, recommended "more time for fellowship -- longer lunch time." (_Newsletter_, Sept. 1963, p. 4.) Robert Storer, Vice President at the time (1963), organized a "Directors' Sharing and Clinic" and said, "We need time for sharing and talk." (_Newsletter_, Sept. 1963, p. 5.) It was not enough to come together in workshops and merely drink in knowledge and ideas. They had to talk things through and reflect on this very special activity known as sacred dance. As was mentioned earlier, Robert Storer was very concerned about the development of sacred dance and the balance between the spiritual and dance technique emphases. In a letter to Mary Jane Wolbers, dated March 7, 1963, Robert thought upon the direction of the Guild. He praised Mary Jane very highly for both her hard working leadership and for her work in sacred dance. But he questioned that the Guild was living out the goals outlined by the original leaders. Robert asked:

> Are we leaving some of us behind? We are a church group. We are not a group trying to make dance religious. We must ask ourselves, 'Better for what? Better dancing for the service of the church for worship, or better dancing for the stage or concert? Which?' We need more down to earth help for our directors, many of whom are not dancers, many of whom have the vision, but need encouragement. Expert technique discourages these people; they are not ready for it . . . I do hope Hanover can be honest and give the public an example of dance as it is used on the chancel and not on a platform. The presentations in New York were interesting. However only the works that could be used on the chancel or in the sanctuary were right for me. We ought to make that stipulation when we invite or accept work for Hanover. It must be suitable for a service of worship . . . How about our June workshop getting some advanced church dance choir people to lead and not another technician unless it happens to be you, Mary Jane, or Leda? We need people who know our people, our leaders, our churches and our problems. . . .We have to start where we are. . . . I am. . .not anywhere

> near where the top modern dancers are, much as I appreciate their work. I do hope I am not holding back progress.

These were some of the thoughts that Bob wanted discussed in some real down to earth talk sessions. He felt the basic identity of the Guild was at stake and that it could drift off into unintended directions by listening more to outside professionals than to inside people. Although one of the main points in his letter was that old tension between advanced technical training and advanced spiritual communication, underlying it all was his concern for the identity of the Guild. "Gab" fests as well as dance fests were in order to mull over many of the tensions and to try to strike a healthy balance.

The particular issue that Bob Storer raised, namely dance training vs. spiritual dedication, reached a high point in the discussion during these years. Because it has been of such basic concern to the Guild, we shall take a close look at two classic statements on this whole issue which appeared in the September 1962 and January 1963 *Newsletters*. A member who signed her name, "Confused", wrote to the editor, and I quote at length:

> I am sympathetic to the Guild's desire

for professional perfection, but I shall never be able to join the dancers in their dance emphasis. . . . Much that the dancers find inspirational and get excited about leaves me cold as far as actual worship is concerned. What they do is good dance, no doubt, and moving, too, but time and again I find myself brought into the presence of God not by their work but rather by the simpler works of groups which thus far seem to receive so much criticism from the professional. For some inexplicable reason the non-professional group is able to project its mood of worship to me more strongly than the group trained by the professional dancer. . . .

Is there a valid place in worship for simpler movements. If it is not dance, I for one shall be perfectly willing to call it something else. Should there be some organization which deals only with the non-professional and his limitations and proceeds on the assumption that, as limited as it is, there is something in it for both the participant and congregation? Does it have to move over into the area of dance -- can't it stay on the simpler level?

In the Sacred Dance Guild it is the dance expert who judges a work. There are no ministers to say 'This is effective or this is not.' Dance experts certainly should judge dance, but I thought we were concerned primarily with worship. I get the impression that the Guild is more concerned about sacred dance as an art form than as a medium of worship. . . .

I owe the Guild a great debt for its original inspiration to me, but the joy and sureness I once felt have given way to a state of confusion. . . . As the Guild goes forward I become increasingly aware of my inadequacies to be doing

> anything whatsoever in this field. At the same time I cannot ignore the fact that creative movement means a lot to me personally and that it meant a lot to my rhythmic choir and congregation. Can the gap between the professional and non-professional ever be closed? Can the Guild meet both needs? (Newsletter, Sept. 1962, p. 11-12.)

To say the least, "Confused" wrote a very impassioned plea. We can surmise that this letter reflected a certain unrest within the Guild at this time. Apparently a number of people felt left behind technically at workshops and came away frustrated. True, there were many levels of dancers and many different kinds of spiritual commitment whthin the Guild, but it seems not all were able to find their place in and their relationship with the organization. Where was the place for the dance novice who felt genuinely inspired to move in a worship context? Where was the challenge for the technically advanced student to explore powerful movement with a risk? At this point in time, the Guild was not able to give sufficient answers to these questions. Basically, the main avenue of creative dance expression was the rhythmic choir in church worship services. Bob Storer's main concern that the dance must be "suitable" for a service of worship left some frustration. What did "suitable" mean? Why only for a service of worship? Although a few were challenging this narrow view of sacred dance, by and large it was accepted, and many struggled and chafed within these bounds. The tension between narrowly defining sacred dance and freely allowing a broad spectrum within the Sacred Dance Guild was increasingly apparent. This problem was tightly interwoven with the whole identity crisis of the Guild; and only today are we beginning to show signs of resolution. As the history of the Sacred Dance Guild has unfolded, a broader outlook in later years has been quite visible. Progressive sacred dancers have experimented with other avenues of expression; and as a result, the rhythmic choir which dances before the altar in the church worship service is not the only means by which one can dance before God. Today, the boundaries and frontiers of sacred dance have been pushed and expanded so that more people can find a place which feels comfortable and has integrity. The Guild of today is reaping the benefits of the seeds that were planted by restless spirits in the early years, seeds which have blossomed and flourished.

Well, the letter from "Confused" opened Pandora's box and had to be answered. In January 1963, Mary Jane Wolbers wrote this open letter which revealed many of her deep feelings for sacred dance:

> . . . the purpose of the Guild . . . 'to provide a means of communication and training for directors of dance choirs, and to stimulate interest in the dance as a religious art form'.
> . . .you are not the only one who is confused. Some of us are confused by a persistent notion . . . that dancers are incapable of approaching a worship experience with any degree of sincerity or reverence, and that their motives in performing are seldom if truly ever "religious".
> We are confused that a church will seek out the (paid) help of professional people (speakers, teachers, artists, musicians, vocalists) and will turn its back on that of the trained dancer.
> We are confused by the rhythmic choir leader who, at the same time rejecting help of professionals, would "lift" the materials of Mary Anthony (or some other professional leader who has served the Guild) and present them to a workshop as her own. . . .
> There are those who feel that the Sacred Dance Guild is divided into two camps, with sincerely religious people on one side and the dancers (who, being strictly exhibitionists, couldn't <u>possibly</u> have any spiritual motivation) on the other . . . . If we are to move, we must learn to move well. To this end we must train. The untrained are reaching out to the trained. The dancers are anxious to deepen their spirituality, to improve their relationship with church people. The Guild is their meeting place. (<u>Newsletter</u>, Jan. 1963, p. 16.)

Among her many other gifts, Mary Jane also has a masterful rhetorical style. The letter from "Confused" obviously hurt the "dancer" and the "spirit" in Mary Jane. She would not accept the implied notion that dancers were less spiritually motivated than non-dancers. Nor would she accept the complacency of the non-dancer to leave her proficiency where it was. Rather, she said, we must all seek to both deepen our spirituality and to increase our dance expertise. The dichotomy should not even exist.

In the same *Newsletter*, Ted Shawn shared some thoughts on this topic; and I quote from him because he was so respected by the Sacred Dance Guild, and he was such a support and inspiration. Also, in his comments, he introduced the notion of congregational dance which will be discussed at great length later, and which, although he did not elaborate on it, is in many ways a partial resolution of this whole debate.

> . . .Sacred Dance can be used in both ways: congregational dance may ultimately be achieved, in which case we do not expect the entire congregation to have training; however, if we do have a choir or soloists, more is expected of them -- and the choir director chooses good voices, well trained voices if possible,

> and he himself is presumably sufficiently trained that he knows good music, and how to produce good music with his trained singers. We ask nothing more of Sacred Dance than this. If any church is going to have a separate group to perform liturgical dance in the church services, then this group must be headed by someone who is himself (herself) sufficiently trained to know how to train others, and we should not be satisfied with inarticulate bodies, wobbling when they walk, and making wooden gestures and trying to look Holy! . . . I have never asked for anything *but* simple movement for use in sacred dance, but anyone knows, who has worked in the field as I have for over fifty years, that simple movement is attained with more difficulty than that which she calls 'professional'. (*Newsletter*, January 1963, p. 17.)

Ted Shawn compared the Sacred Dance choir with the singing choir. Just as we would expect a trained director for the singing choir, so we should for the dancing choir. And just as we should expect a vocal soloist to have a trained voice, so we should expect a dance soloist to have a trained body. He also clarified the mistaken notion that "professional" was antithetical to "simple". Simplicity in the chancel did not mean one did not require training. Quite the contrary. Lack of training could turn "simple" into trite and repetitive. If one is going to perform, then one should prepare through disciplined training, and not look for a short-cut just because it is a "spiritual" activity. But, even for the untrained mover there was a way. Ted's words, "congregational dance may ultimately be achieved," ring out like the words of a prophet; for today this has been achieved. Untrained people can dance in the congregation just as everyone sings the hymns during the service.

The editor, Margaret Fisk Taylor, summed up the letters in her usual balanced fashion, noting the variety within the Sacred Dance Guild and sensing that, "We are in a _burst_ of new creative explorations." (_Newsletter_, January 1963, p. 18.) There would still be confusion, the debate was certainly not closed; but this particular airing of the problem was needed both for clarification and for representation of some of the tensions among Guild members. Today, we still have those varieties of people, but the polarization does not appear to exist at nearly the same intensity, if at all. The Guild, I believe, is successfully resolving this long standing problem.

Aside from the particular debate we have just examined, let us look at some of the statements made at this time on sacred dance in general, and then some of the special activities of some members that helped the

Guild to stretch and grow.

Margaret Fisk Taylor, editor during these years, shared some thoughts in almost every issue of the _Newsletter_. Very gently and never with judgment she held out to the members of the Guild fresh vision of religious dance. Never stagnant in her own personal development, she led the Guild along with her as she grew in her own understanding of sacred dance. Margaret was aware of the immaturity of many members and encouraged them to try very honestly to communicate their own experience -- including their flounderings. Sacred dance must be more than just "pretty". She admonished:

> Has your Rhythmic Choir or Sacred Dance Choir been drifting in a blissful haze? Before your choir expresses conviction or serenity, let them admit their frustrations, bewilderment, and agony. You must go the "first mile" honestly -- admitting anxiety, hostility, etc. before you are ready for the "second mile" of sharing fragments of meaningful insights. . . . In our Sacred Dance Guild may there be: variety and integrity . . . vision and conviction . . . disciplined skill and creative exploration . . . identity with agony and sharing fragments of faith in the midst of agony . . . awareness of the eternal and confrontation with the now. (_Newsletter_, Sept. 1962, p. 13.)

Although some persons confessed to being

untrained and they rather naively set up the dichotomy between the "dancer" and the "religious" in the Sacred Dance Guild, they showed efforts to be thinking, sensitive directors of sacred dance. Their understanding of the irony of "stillness" expressed through motion was extremely profound.

Another contribution to the collection of thinking in the Guild came from the Rabbi Milton Richman who submitted a very helpful essay to the Newsletter in January, 1964. Sharing Biblical research he had done which would aid modern sacred dance, he formed three categories: "gesture" -- performed entirely by the hands; "attitude" -- performed by the body; and "movement" -- performed in more than body space. In the Bible he found specific examples which would fit under each of these three categories. Under "gesture", he found:

> Spreading the hands; Lifting the hands; Clapping the hand; Holding out the hands and waving them; Raising the hand over someone or something; Laying on the hands on someone or something; Touching with the hands someone or something.
> Of body attitudes we find: Facing the body toward; Bowing and prostrating the body toward; Kneeling; Kissing someone or something.
> Of movements we find: Dancing with people and instruments in rhythmic forms; Dancing

> with leaping alone; Ecstatic movements done individually though together with others, with instruments. (*Newsletter*, January 1964, p. 6.)

Rabbi Richman felt the sacred dancer could recapture the Biblical sense of harmony between man, God and the world, and the sense of prayer as a total response of body and soul. His careful analysis of Scripture served to help build a solid base on which members could "dance". It gave the Guild a little more confidence. Essays such as his were tremendously helpful to the understanding of the Biblical sanction of religious dance.

Besides the obvious contributions of articles and essays to the growth of the Guild, a more subtle illustration of its direction was in the section entitled, "What our members are doing." In the first few years, this section was very small, but by 1962 it had grown considerably beyond the entries of the Guild leaders alone. Members from all over the States were beginning to share their activities. And it was this sharing that counted most in pushing the boundaries of the Sacred Dance Guild to a point where it could contain the many varieties of expressions of sacred dance. In fact, by 1965 in the February meeting, a statement was formulated to broaden the Guild's description of sacred dance to include dance in art and religious education <u>and rehabilitation</u>. Three years earlier in the April 1962 issue of the <u>Newsletter</u>, Nels Anderson from Michigan had sent in a very short note that among other things said he was working with a group of retarded children once a week. In January 1964, Leda Canino of New York said that her most interesting work was with crippled children in an orthopedic hospital and with teenagers who had been neglected or orphaned. Dance Therapy was beginning to have a great deal of influence on the Sacred Dance Guild. In September 1964, Mary Jane Wolbers reported that she had attended a seminar on "Dance Education for the Deaf", and the following year Mary Jane became the liason between the Sacred Dance Guild and Dance Therapists. In the summer of 1965, Paula Gold of Oklahoma wrote a manual of creative rhythmic movement for the mentally retarded. She had twelve retarded persons in her movement choir, ages twenty to fifty-eight -- an unprecedented achievement. That same summer, the first clinic in dance education for the handicapped was held in Dayton, Ohio.

Other items of a special nature that were listed in this section, "What our members are doing", included: a number of theses being written in the area of sacred dance; a note from Mary Jane Wolbers on congregational response in dance; a seventy-five member rhythmic choir, one of the leaders of which was a County Probation Department Counsellor; themes current to the sixties such as civil rights, women, memorials to the war dead and to John F. Kennedy. It appears that many members were doing exactly what Margaret Fisk Taylor had hoped -- they were attempting to reflect the agony of those troubled times. This section of the Newsletter has been a very keen barometer which has measured the growth and development of the Guild.

These years of 1962-1965 appear at first glance to be declining years. If one looked only at the lack of organization and cooperation the situation did seem dismal, but I suggest these were important growing years, which saw the development of the identity of the Guild and the increase in the understanding of the nature and importance of sacred dance. These were very difficult years for the leadership of the Guild; and it felt to many they were not really moving ahead at all. But the Guild did grow numerically, geographically, and philosophically in its concept of what constituted sacred dance.

CHAPTER III

1966-1968

Into the Sacred Dance Guild with its interesting mixture of growth and stagnation, entered a highly unusual leader with qualities which were to give it new life and direction. Pat Sonen became President in 1966. A creative, progressive fire ball of energy, Pat led the Guild on a route that almost completely changed its structure. In her presidential message of her last year of office, in February 1968, Pat said, "This may be the last year the Sacred Dance Guild exists _as we know it_!" (_Newsletter_, February 1968, p. 7.) That was a radical prophecy that was backed up by two years of hard work, inspired and driven by Pat herself. The radical changes did not then take place; but the proposals were carefully thought out and have guided recent changes.

The basic plan (not entirely new to the Guild) was to re-organize into chapters throughout the entire country. The format was finalized at an over-night executive meeting that Pat called in November. It was so like Pat to plan this meeting the way she did -- enticing board members to a retreat in the mountains with lots of delicious food and business with a new approach. The board came and the rewards of fellowship and accomplishment were shared in the February 1968 Newsletter.

The agenda for that historic Board Meeting was basically a study of the possibilities for re-structuring the Sacred Dance Guild. The Board proposed that the Guild have three vice presidents to act as area directors in the east, mid-west, and west and to facilitate regional development. Chapters would be formed with a minimum of twenty members. Regional directors would have increased responsibility in communicating with local churches, seminaries, etc.; in compiling a local mailing list to be shared with the corresponding secretary; and to promote small local workshops as well as regional workshops. A chapter could be formed by a group of twenty or more members applying to the National Executive Board. With approval, officers would be elected with the chairman automatically becoming a member of the National Board. Chapters would have to meet a minimum of once a year; and the "Annual" meeting of the Sacred Dance Guild would be held only once every two years. Dues would be collected at the chapter level, except for members at large; and part of the dues would be sent to the National Board, part kept by the local chapter for program expenses.

Two distinct purposes for organizing into chapters were presented. The first was to "stimulate growth of the Sacred Dance Guild at the grass roots level through increased programming and enlarged membership." (Newsletter, Feb. 1968, 1. 9.) The size of the Guild had been increasing only very slowly, because, although many new ones joined every year, unfortunately many also dropped their membership. This has been a persistent problem for the Guild over the years and it was hoped that tighter local units would encourage people to maintain their membership. Of course workshops often were the occasion for signing up new members; so any increase in programming would help the Guild in that area.

The second purpose as stated in the Newsletter was to "enable the National Executive Board to become a creative body by releasing it from mechanical duties." (Newsletter, February 1968, p. 9.) The National Board could then concentrate on clarifying the purpose and goals of the Guild, enlarge its stature and dignity, raise much needed funds, and be a resource to the local chapters.

A mail ballot was included in the Newsletter. In June, one of the most radical steps the Guild had ever attempted was about to be taken. But -- it did not happen. Shortly before the June meeting, Pat lost her husband, the Reverend Robert Sonen, and she was absent from the meeting. What exactly did happen is not clear. A vote was taken,but there was no amendment of the By-laws to officially initiate the necessary action. Thus, the attempt aborted and the plans were temporarily laid aside. Consequently, the Guild hesitated. But the groundwork for change was not in vain. The passionate vision Pat shared in 1968 is particularly compelling even today, since the Guild is presently growing most strongly at the grass roots level. Copies of the organizational chart drawn up by Pat and her committee were still being passed around to Board members in 1978 along with the question, "Is now the time?" The planning and research have been thoroughly done for the reorganization of the Guild. A fine set of blue prints have been passed down by the Sonen administration and have been partly adopted in 1978.

While these new ideas concerning reorganization were being discussed, of course the Sacred Dance Guild continued to grow slowly and mature. By 1967, there were at least two hundred active sacred dance choirs in the United States. (Newsletter, January 1967, p.11) To help spread the word of the existence of the

Guild, a brochure was finally prepared in September 1966, thanks to Board member Judith Bennett. The reader will recall that this Brochure had been stalled in previous years because many felt there was not a clear picture of the organization. The long-awaited publication was a subtle but fair indication that the Guild had a better sense of identity, and that it could boast of its contribution to the religious art world. Not long after this time, a travelling publicity exhibit was prepared with pictures, brochures, literature, program flyers, etc. on a large cloth which could be hung at workshops. This gave a fuller and more intimate introduction to the Guild and some of its members. Communication and healthy exposure were of paramount importance, and those with vision explored as many ways as possible that the message of the Guild could be shared. As National Publicity Chairman at the time, Judy Bennett stated that one of the major responsibilities of the Sacred Dance Guild was education of the public.

Besides the need to publicize and educate the public outside the Guild, there was also the need to experiment with more sophisticated methods of sharing ideas and choreographies within the Guild. The possibility of a film library of religious dance was discussed. Drid Williams, a leader of several workshops during these years, filmed "Kinescope Anonyme", one of her choreographic works. She encouraged the Guild to make high calibre material available to members to help raise the vision of what could be accomplished. Unfortunately film making is an expensive venture; and the Guild has not had the funds to sponsor such an undertaking. Only a few professional individuals have had some of their works filmed or videotaped; and even these have received sparse circulation within the Guild.

Many progressive ideas such as this fell on the ears of a Guild emerging out of a limited view of sacred dance into a broader one. In her opening Presidential message in 1966, Pat Sonen included among her goals the expansion of the Guild's use of the term "sacred dance". She hoped that a more liberal outlook would attract more dancers and creative movers into the Guild. One question raised by some members was, "Should sacred dance be done only in the church?" Bob Storer had influenced the thought on this issue in the earlier years, but more individuals were now saying that religious dance in a theatre was as powerful as that in the sanctuary. Members were striking out in new directions; and they needed the respect and dignity which the more traditional dancers had. Believing that breadth would strengthen the Guild, Pat Sonen encouraged a more liberal approach. She welcomed those who respected the purpose and direction of the Guild even though they perhaps did not do the typically accepted thing.

And, realistically speaking, the breadth was already apparent among the members. Dance Therapy was gaining wider attention in the dance world at large, and so it was in the Sacred Dance Guild. Pat Harper of Michigan reported doing a Christmas program for children in the orthopedics section of a hospital, "encouraging the handicapped children to use their upper bodies to join with her in movement to "Away in a Manger'." (Newsletter, February 1968, p. 16.) In May of 1968, due to the increasing interest of many Sacred Dance Guild members in dance therapy, comments on a book, and a time to dance, by Norma Canner and Harriet Klebanoff, published by Beacon Press, were reported by The Boston Globe:

> In the dance groups, some children who were not previously known to speak have been able to communicate through words. Others, far removed in a private lonely world, have learned to touch, and to

> reach out for the touch of another person. (*Newsletter*, May 1968, p. 13.)

The healing power of movement was fully recognized. But, the potential was only beginning to be tapped. A completely valid ministry in dance, the field of healing was opened up; and the reports that trickled into the *Newsletter* were warm and compassionate and open. The good news was that people were now not only being moved, they were experiencing healing.

That deep sense of being "called" into a ministry of dance was described by Guild member Pixie Hammond, of California. She shared a very personal experience in which she received her call into sacred dance. She wrote an unassuming, very moving article for the *Newsletter* called "Praise the Lord with the Dance", and symbolized the humility of the dancer along with the conviction of one who praises God completely with body and soul:

> My own first experience with dance in worship took place years ago in the privacy of my own bedroom. I had just read a book (Margaret Fisk Taylor's "The Art of the Rhythmic Choir") and was so thrilled with the idea, I decided to try it right then and there. In the back of the book were directions (by Evelyn Broadbent) for interpreting the Lord's Prayer. I knelt on the floor, the open book in

> front of me and folded my hands. "Our Father," I raised my eyes. . . . "Hallowed be Thy name," I bowed low, and something trembled within me. . . . "For Thine is the Kingdom," I extended my arms, filled with wonder that so simple a movement could make His presence so real. "And the power, and the Glory." A strange strength lifted my heart. As I folded my hands for the amen, and knelt again, I knew that while some are called to preach, others to teach, that I had been called to dance. It was a deeply moving religious experience, and, to this day, I consider dance a sacred calling. (Newsletter, September 1966, p. 17-18)

A beautiful description of a beautiful moment. The very interesting thing is that the movement made the prayer alive for her. Initially she was merely going to try something that intrigued her; but in a mysterious way, movement reached down into her soul and blessed her with the Presence of God. Later in her article, Pixie spoke to the issue of religious devotion and technical proficiency and very gently stated that both should be present at a very high degree:

> This requires a combination of skill in movement and a deep spiritual dedication. . . .The movements alone, no matter how skilled, will not carry the message. Religious devotion, no matter how sincere, cannot make up for a sloppy performance. . . .We can expect the director and choir members alike to be willing to work at the skills of their art. . . . Wherever

> did we get the idea that if it is to be presented in church it can be second-rate? Religious art is a gift of God -- how dare it be less than the best? . . .Our first aim is to grow spiritually, and dance is simply the expression of this seeking. . . .I try to devote about half of our rehearsal time to prayer, meditation, and theological discussions. . . .When we really discover His Spirit within us, we can't keep from praising Him with words, with music, with drama -- and with dance! (Newsletter, Sept. 1966, p. 18.)

This article was perhaps one of the most balanced offerings on this trying issue. It was challenging and uplifting at the same time -- a real tribute to the development of thought and inspiration on the part of the members of the Guild.

A few months later, Margaret Fisk Taylor wrote an editorial to describe her attempt at balance for members of the Sacred Dance Guild:

> I have tried to maintain balance in SACRED-DANCE as a hyphenated concept: not (sacred) DANCE nor SACRED (dance). The material in the Newsletter and the leadership at Sacred-Dance Guild Workshops should offer a healthy balance in content (provocative concerns), vision (purpose) and dance (movement tools for communicating). Dancers need exposure to contemporary religious emphases and church groups need exposure to dance empases. It can be

> enrichment both ways -- an art discipline and a spiritual discipline interfused. (Newsletter, Sept. 1967, p. 1.)

Margaret was the perfect person to be editor of the Newsletter during these years, and the Guild was privileged that she remained on the job for so long. A pioneer in sacred dance, she continued to forge ahead as she sensed the direction of this movement. Always fresh in her approach, Margaret inspired the Guild with new insights, and gave it a sense of solidarity with her words of wisdom.

The years 1966-1968 were another watershed in the history of the Sacred Dance Guild. The contagious enthusiasm and optimistic vision of President Pat Sonen transformed the Guild into a self-confident orgainization with the potential to make a powerful contribution to the world. Her presidential messages raised the readers' level of energy, belief, and joy. She inspired pride in the Sacred Dance Guild because she was proud of it and was committed to its purpose. Her immediate dream of restructuring the Guild was not realized -- in fact it left her disillusioned as shall be discussed in the next chapter -- but perhaps she was only a little ahead of her time. Her vision is more of a lively option today than ever. But beyond her specific plans, Pat Sonen became a model in her dedication, zeal, and brilliant sense of prophecy.

CHAPTER IV

1968-1974

The years following the climactic endeavor completely to restructure the Sacred Dance Guild into regional chapters were years of reshuffling and re-examination. The Guild seemed somewhat in a state of limbo. Pat Sonen remained President until June of 1969. Her final "Presidential Patter" as she called it, appeared in the May Newsletter; and it was not the victorious farewell that readers expected from Pat. Her "bounce" was missing from the message; and in its place was a note of sadness and disillusionment. She opened her message with, "This is the time for me to say certain things -- certain 'expected' things." (Newsletter, May 1969, p. 2.) And she did -- briefly. But, then very quickly she moved on to questions like, "What about those times when people wouldn't help? . . .What about the people who said they would do a job, and never were able to?" (Newsletter, May 1969, p. 2.) These were harsh, distressed words, reminiscent of similar phrases in a letter from Mary Jane Wolbers, already quoted in Chapter III. To her successor, Pat wrote:

> What is usually said? Oh, yes, I pass on to my successor a dream begun -- but a dream that needs to pick up steam and be expanded and to lead this organization on to what is should be. Take it -- and bless you. (Newsletter, May 1969, p. 2.)

Pat dreamed for the Guild and gave herself to that dream. But, by the end of her presidency, Pat could see only what had not been accomplished. It was a difficult thing to work so hard for something she believed in and not have the joy of seeing it materialize. The organizational machinery at the top was still not able to facilitate the increasing business of the Guild. The problems of lack of co-operation, leaders who did not carry out their responsibilities properly, and a president carrying too much of the burden alone made the Sacred Dance Guild entirely too top heavy. The tumble that followed 1968 would affect profoundly the subsequent years. When Virginia Lucke took over in 1970, she was very distressed by the many gaps of information on the history of the Sacred Dance Guild and the complete void after 1967. She was not even sure what happened to the By-laws revisions presented in 1968. The legacy to Margaret Fisk Taylor, Virginia Lucke, and Maxine DeBruyn who were the presidents during the period 1969-1974 was a very mixed one. The intensity of the work on the by-laws, under Pat Sonen, had not been equalled at any other time. The proposals by the committee had been clear and specific with only details and execution remaining to be handled. But ingredients were missing; and it was the responsibility of the leadership of the next few years to discover what those ingredients were.

The organizational difficulties were obvious indeed. But, on the positive side, the subsequent presidents inherited an exciting Guild membership that was growing and developing and stretching the boundaries. In her Presidential message, Margaret Fisk Taylor saw where the future of the Guild would be decided, "The officers can do very little; the growing edge is with each one of you just where you live and in what you do with this dynamic art of sacred dance." (Newsletter, Fall 1969, p. 2.) In a sense, the leadership was passing the ball back to the membership. The leaders would have to learn to "listen" very carefully to sense the direction in which the Guild was ready to go.

There were many examples of that "growing edge" to which Margaret referred. The West was opening up very well. Virginia Lucke wrote in a letter in October 1969, "Michigan is fairly bustin' out all over with enthusiasm for dance." Connie Fisher from Colorado wrote to the Fall 1969 Newsletter:

> I have never taught so many workshops in one period of time. . . . The people here, of all denominations, have accepted the new forms of worship with open arms and one year's work has only begun to scratch the surface. (Newsletter, Fall 1969, p. 10.)

The Spring 1974 Newsletter reported the South West was really coming alive: the first national Guild workshop west of the Mississippi was held in Phoenix, Arizona. What a landmark! A sense of pride and independence from the East was growing.

In the meantime, members continued to send their various notices of creative activity. More theses on dance in Christian liturgy were being written. (Newsletter, Spring 1972, p. 9.) Historical plays with dance, such as the "Play of Herod" from the twelfth century, were being produced. Robert Yohn, a professional dancer from New York, and a leader at many sacred dance workshops in the seventies, had his "Testaments Seen and Heard" filmed with the help of the Sacred Dance Guild. (Newsletter, Fall 1971, p. 5.) (Virginia Lucke said in a letter that the Sacred Dance Guild needed an "angel" to fund the filming of religious dance films.) Lane Boswell, from Rockville Center, N.Y., danced with her infant son at his baptism on Mothers' Day. (Newsletter, Spring 1971, p.15.) Clem Burton, of Ohio, took his rhythmic choir on a tour in Japan in conjunction with a program called PROMISES. (Newsletter, Spring 1971, p. 16.) A few titles of religious dance programs took on very unusual twists such as, "God .. or .. How Evolution Transformed the Chocolate Bar". (Newsletter, Fall 1973, p.17.) An entry by Vira Klawe, director of the Huntington Dancers of Faith, in Long Island, revealed some of the varieties of dance that members were exploring. In one program, her group performed: 'pre-Christian Harvest Dance of Ancient Israel, through the Sun-Worshippers of Peru, Dervishes of Early Persia, prayer dances of India, Psalms of the Old Testament, and a modern example to Godspell music." (Newsletter, Spring 1972, p. 14.)

And in the area of dance for the handicapped, many new fronts were being explored. After being approached by the local Industrial Home for the Blind, Lane Boswell's group from Long Island looked into the possibility of teaching modern dance to a group of blind teenagers. (Newsletter, Fall 1973, p. 22.)

In Washington, D.C., the Gallaudet Dancers from the School of the Deaf presented a full program of dance in worship at the Luther Place Memorial Church in the Fall of 1974. (Newsletter, Winter 1974-75, p. 21.) All of these events are really quite astounding achievements in the history of the Guild! They reveal wide-open, creative thinking and the willingness to experiment among the members of the Guild. They were far from narrow in their approach and with each issue of the Newsletter, the way was widened even more. Members used the Newsletter very well and were very willing to share their good news with fellow members through this most vital link in communication. They were increasingly aware that what they did was important; and, reflecting an attitude of growing self-confidence, the sharing of activities across the country snowballed. This sharing of news would have a great influence on the future of the Guild.

Two specific dance innovations made their appearance in the Guild during these years. Because of their increasing popularity today, they require some special attention. One is Sufi Dance. Several Guild members began to send in news of sufi dancing from all parts of the country. In the Fall 1973 Newsletter, exerpts from the Sufi Quarterly were quoted to give members some understanding of the origins of sufi dance:

> The Whirling dervishes are a sect of Islamic mystics called 'Mevlevi' founded in Konya, Turkey in the 13th century . . . They adhere to the fundamental mystical concept that the divine inheres in human beings and that a human being can achieve union with the divine by divesting himself of all ties to 'self' and 'this world'. Their rites lay a heavy emphasis on poetry, music and a peculiar whirling dance, the combined effects of which produce trance-like states in which the dervish experiences an altered and/or heightened perception. (Newsletter, Fall 1973, p. 14-15.)

The whirling dance is one particular type of of dance among Sufi followers. Savitri Popkin from Pennsylvania, who has a Doctorate in Dance with special interest in Sufism, has led Guild members in several types of circle dances. A group will join hands to form a circle and travel the circular path with a simple combination of movements while respectively singing short verses of praise to God. The internal effect on the individual is much like that of the whirling dance, that is, a heightened perception. The reason for singing the chants over and over again is that they vibrate the energy centers of the body, raising the energy into the higher spheres while creating cosmic harmonies. The repetition of the movement firmly implants the dance so that it becomes automatic. This allows the Spirit to enter each person, because she or he become a clear channel for the transmission of the divine. The total experience reminds one somewhat of meditation. But in the case of Sufi Dance, the simple movements and chants are the vehicle for the elevation of the whole person. It has been such a short time since Sufi Dance has been introduced to the Guild that it is difficult to evaluate its influence. It will be discussed further in the next chapter.

The second innovation within the Guild during these years is "congregational dance". It was first mentioned in the Newsletter back in 1962 in a little note by Mary Jane Wolbers in which she referred to congregational response in dance. But, starting in 1969, reports about dance involving congregational participation sprinkled through the activity reports from across the nation and the world. Doug Adams, presently Professor at Pacific School of Religion in Berkeley, California, is largely responsible for this. In the Newsletter of May 1969, Doug wrote that, "Seminary students at Pacific School of Religion . . .participated in a four-day experiment in involving congregations in worship as Margaret Fisk Taylor led their one-hour chapel periods." (Newsletter, May 1969, p. 13.) From Massachusetts, Naomi Aleh-Leaf, a leader at several Sacred Dance Guild workshops in dances of the Near East, wrote in the same Newsletter that in her work she expected, "to be involving the congregants in more movement and participation." (Newsletter, May 1969, p. 14.) (Again, it is remarkable that there were two notes on this particular subject of congregational dance in the same Newsletter. The reader will observe that this "coincidence" has happened with a number of issues which made their first appearance in the Newsletter; but from more than one source. One cannot help but think of the Scripture: "When two or three are gathered . . .)

Since the Spring of 1969, almost every Newsletter has had some mention of congregational dance. Gradually, members gained the confidence to invite the congregation to join the dancers in some non-threatening way. This was very risky for both leaders and congregation. The safety of "performing" and being in total control was very secure, and an adventurous spirit was required to release that security. After all, what if it did not work? The result could be chaos. But, as more reports of successful attempts appeared in the *Newsletter*, more members did give it a try. Reports such as this one began to come in more and more frequently: in Phoenix, Arizona, at the Cross Roads United Methodist Church, Betty Johnson's Dance Choir "led a congregation of five hundred in moving to Psalm 150." (*Newsletter*, Fall 1969, p. 9.) That is a lot of people to lead in a meaningful fashion.

Meanwhile, Doug was experimenting freely with all the dimensions of congregational dance. He actually encouraged *spontaneous* dance by the congregation in some parts of the service: "Pews are sometimes pushed back to make room for dance. At times, stanzas and chorus are rehearsed before the service to permit alternate dance roles while others sing." (*Newsletter*, Fall 1969, p. 9.) At other times Doug used concentric circles around the communion table. Pulling together many of his ideas and experiences, in 1972 Doug wrote a book, *Congregational Dancing in Christian Worship*, which has become a popular handbook for anyone interested in the subject. He dedicated it to Margaret Fisk Taylor for, "She is truly the one who has inspired many of us to explore full participation of the whole congregation in movement." (*Newsletter*,

Winter 1972, p. 9.) So, again we come back to Margaret. Throughout all the years of the Sacred Dance Guild, and indeed for many years preceding, Margaret Fisk Taylor has been our pioneer _par excellence_, a woman with vision and with that quiet yet dynamic ability to inspire.

As can be seen, therefore, at the grass roots level, there was definitely an attitude of anticipation and experimentation. The Guild was a moving organism. In the midst of it all, however, the leaders were still having to wrestle with the difficult business of the organization and planning. An item in the minutes of the June 1969 meeting reported the need for regional workshops -- a somewhat anachronistic note after all the high-powered planning for regional chapters during the preceding two years. Indeed, a lot of fronts begged for attention; but behind them all was that need for a sense of identity and a sense of pride. Members needed to feel that _they_ were the Sacred Dance Guild. In order to invest in the future of the Guild, the Ruby Henderson Memorial Fund (which had been formed back in 1962), needed to be increased. It was intended to help promising youngsters who might be future leaders in the Guild to attend the annual Institute. To help build it up, it was suggested that profits from workshops, both Guild sponsored and local could be funnelled into the Scholarship Fund. But without a sense of pride and belonging, that suggestion could not really be taken seriously. Today, there are all the signs that both Guild pride and commitment are growing.

A very helpful development during these years which certainly helped to improve the Guild's self-identity was the recognition of the Sacred Dance Guild by other dance circles. In July 1973, for the first time, the Guild was represented at Dance Congress. And in the Spring of 1974, for the second year in a row, Mary Jane Wolbers represented the Sacred Dance Guild at the Forum of National Dance Organizations. Mary Jane reported:

> It is interesting to have had the privilege of meeting with the Forum and see the awareness of the Sacred Dance Guild grow at the national level. Members are eager to learn what we are doing, to share in our concerns, and to report names and addresses of interested persons to us. (Newsletter, Fall 1974-1975, p. 9.)

It was very encouraging to know that dancers in general felt that the Sacred Dance Guild was doing an important work and that they were interested in its development.

Within the Guild as well, there were indicators of how it felt about its own work. To conclude this section we will examine some statements and articles in the Newsletter which reflect some of the current thinking. It will be apparent from the diversity that these years were a period of flux, of searching, and of a rising strength among the members of the Guild.

The relationship of dancers with the congregation was one of the major issues, both at the level of educating the public on what sacred dance is, and actually involving the public in the dance. There were those whose experience told them it was practically hopeless. A rather cynical note was struck by Judy Bennett in an open letter to Harvey Cox, a response to his recent book, Feast of Fools:

> I'm just plain battle-weary. There have been moments of satisfaction, of exultation, of joy, it's true, but after four years on the road and another eleven before that of involvement in dance-in-the-church in various forms, I've got a few scars on my psyche to match the aches in my muscles. You see, they don't really understand us out there, Dr. Cox. . . . And everything is peaches and cream kind of a dance -- . . . a pretty dance! Only trouble is, life's not always pretty, and I want to dance about life, and offer that dance to God, but

> it's hard to do that in the church because there's no market there for dances with . . . GUTS. . . . I used to be concerned about the quality of my work; now I'm forced to be preoccupied with its acceptability, its inoffensiveness. . . . But I won't, as a dancer, compromise what I know to be worthy and true just to pacify church ladies with "body-hangups". I'll dance somewhere else first. . . . I hope you're right, Dr. C. -- about the return of festivity and the affirmation of the flesh in the house of God -- I hope you're right and that we've just been dancing in the wrong churches. And if you're not, well then, we'll hope that the time you wrote about will arrive soon, when "once again we can talk about the redemption of the body without embarrassment." (Newsletter, Spring 1970, p. 2, 9-10.)

This was the only such letter that ever appeared in the Newsletter, but it did point up very strongly some of the problems that sacred dancers faced from time to time. Judy's group wanted to experiment in contemporary music and themes but could not seem to communicate beyond the "tsk, tsk" of "church ladies with body-hangups." Judy, in a most vivid and rhetorical fashion brought to the attention of the Guild the important question of how much a sacred dance choir should pacify the conservative in the pew and how much the choir should forge ahead to challenge the congregation.

In a letter to Virginia Lucke, Jean Gal of Michigan, in February 1970, reflected the tension of the sacred dancer who as a true artist should be a prophet or leader in spiritual understanding: "Can one continue to genuflect and lift arms and eyes heavenward year after year and be effective --? That of course may be simplistic -- but it may be worth discussing." The problem of using movements that were recognizable and meaningful to the congregation and yet new and fresh at the same time was very deep and challenging -- not to mention frustrating when faced with conservatism. More than one Guild member has had to deal with that terrible, thankfully rare, moment when someone from the congregation has stood up and hollered "Sacriligious!" or some such word in the midst of the dancing. That has been the risk of dancers in the church.

At the other extreme of Judy Bennett's frustration at not having the freedom to dance as she wanted or to use the costumes and music she felt were necessary was an article by Sister Mary Aquin Chester. Titled, "Creative Movement Within the Liturgy", it described her experience: "Our efforts at St. Mary Motherhouse Chapel to develop symbolic gesture within the liturgy have been guided by the following priciple stated by our chaplain: start with the gestures that are already called for in the liturgy.: (Newsletter, May 1969, p. 10.) She then reviewed two dances, the Palm Sunday Procession and the ceremonies of the Easter Vigil, which utilized the basic liturgy and only subtly but dramatically elaborated on the movements. It was well received even by those who were not sympathetic to dance as a part of the liturgy. Her approach was very basic and very careful. It was her way of handling a potentially negative reaction from a conservative congregation.

Stated simply, the problem has been to reconcile the progressive experimental spirit of the dancer with the conservative spirit of some congregations. In an indirect way, exerpts from an article, Emphases of Israelite Dancers, by Doug Adams in the May 1969 Newsletter throws some light on this discussion:

> An emphasis in Israelite dance to divine union was that coming to God included coming together with fellow men. This emphasis is revealed in the fact that one did not dance alone but rather danced in a band or circle with others. . . . Thus there is no sharp distinction between

> dance to divine union and dance as a means to community and greater commitment to the world. (Newsletter, May 1969, p. 11.)

This is a subtle, but extremely profound statement. As Doug explained, Israelite dancing accomplished a two-fold need: union with God and a sense of community with one's neighbor. In fact, these two were really one. They could not be separated. What does this have to say to sacred dancers? -- that the sense of community must not take second place to, or be separated from, the liturgical dance. This basic rule should allow for experimentation and renewal, but does not permit divisiveness.

Doug Adams has suggested that movement is integral to a sense of community. At a United Church conference on new forms of worship held in northern California, Doug described his thoughts on the use of dance in worship:

> The word becomes flesh and brings joy to the world. As the religion of the incarnation, we ought to have more incarnation in our worship. Our God is an active, moving God: yet in our worship service, we sit still, or try to. And then we wonder why a sense of community and joy are often missing in our Protestant pew-centered worship. One reason

> that so many fail to find community and joy in the worship is that instead of moving, they sit. We as ministers and choir members may find a great sense of community and joy in worship; but we are often the only ones who are moving. In the Hebrew language "company" is derived from "dance"; and in the Aramaic which Jesus spoke, "dance" is the basis for "rejoicing". Thus, Jesus tells us, "Rejoice and leap for joy." (Luke 6:23). . . . The early church did a great deal of dancing -- incarnating the words of the gospel and hymns. The words "choir" and "carol" and "chorus" derive from "dance". . . .Latin for bishop (praesul) meant "dance leader". Pews and pulpits and other obstructions to movement are very recent additions to churches and are rarely to be found in the Orthodox areas of Christianity. . . .Rows of pews (which in the early Church were few in numbers and reserved for the aged and infirm) are a sad testimony to the vitality of Christianity in the West today. . . . Let us move our souls off ice. . . . Let us move our mind-body-souls into action. (In Dante's vision as with many in literature, the closer one is to God the more active one becomes: the angels are led by God in dance; and so, let us dance.) (Newsletter, Spring 1970, p. 13.)

Doug followed this theoretical discourse with simple practical suggestions that could easily be implemented in the worship service. I have quoted Doug at length to give the reader the flavor of his writing and enough of his argument to understand clearly his motivation and this direction. Doug said that we have stunted our worship and have thereby stunted our community. Congregational movement would be a vehicle for creating community and worshipping God at the same time.

By 1974, Doug was suggesting that:

> . . .the question is no longer whether there will be dance within worship but rather what dances are appropriate at which moments of worship to express the particular liturgy. (Newsletter, Spring 1973-1974, p. 9.)

That is a radical statement, even for the Sacred Dance Guild! Doug was saying that dance should not be an unusual ingredient in worship but should be a regular occurrence. Compare his view with the philosophy of the Reverend Robert Storer as quoted in a master's thesis by Marilyn Kay Lewis Hart, "A Study of Modern Dance as a Means of Worship in the United States with Emphasis upon the History, Development, and Contributions of the Sacred Dance Guild and of Rhythmic Choirs", written in 1965:

> It is not my thought that this kind of dancing can or should replace our present forms of worship, or that it should be a regular part of Sunday services.

> I am convinced that rhythmic work can enrich our present forms of pageantry, that it can be used for processionals and occasionally to interpret an anthem. I am likewise convinced that the practice of rhythm is most beneficial to the young people who participate. (Newsletter, Winter 1974-1975, p. 8.)

This statement is from the opposite end of the spectrum from that by Doug Adams. Both men are ministers, one very active in the early years of the Guild, the other the current president. They hold two radically opposed views -- the Reverend Robert Storer recommended sacred dance as a periodical enrichment of the worship service; the Reverend Doug Adams recommended that our present forms of worship are inadequate and that dance should be a regular integral part of worship. Ironically, in essence, both of these views were concerned with the integrity of the church service and with the challenge of building community. Yet both arrived at opposite conclusions -- in part due to the different times in which they spoke.

Over the years, the Guild has been well represented by a myriad of thoughtful serious dancers who have wanted and expected the best in sacred dance. L'Ana Hyams of Syosset,

New York, a serious ballet dancer and one for whom the religious dimension was of profound importance, wrote several items for the <u>Newsletter</u> in which she shared her deep concern for good, careful sacred dance. Here is a sample:

> Sacred Dance is too important and wonderful to be treated thoughtlessly, and somewhat naively, which seems to be when people want to stick it in everywhere. There is a certain attitude attached to those who approach sacred dance in that manner. It makes me feel that I am talking about a different sacred dance than they are. If we do not become more serious, sacred dance is going to become a very surface and commercialized slogan. We all want to share the miracle and joy we have found in dance, no matter what the level, but rushing into it over-enthusiastically destroys that deep down truth we want to share. For something which is sacred, a great deal of preparation, understanding, and thought are needed before you can expect to <u>really</u> share a part of yourself, and that amazing power of God within you. (<u>Newsletter</u>, Winter 1974-1975, p. 19.)

L'Ana's words were representative of many in the Guild who said we must proceed with our best, with that which is borne out of the depths of our creative beings that it may become a true sharing in the worship service. Anything less is destructive to the community.

In 1972, one of the prime mentors of the Sacred Dance Guild in its early years, Ted Shawn, died. He was a giant in the entire dance world at large and was a very special member of the Guild. In the Spring of that year, a portion of his creed (which remains one of the most stunning and prophetic cogent statements on dance) was quoted in the Newsletter. His words are an appropriate conclusion to this chapter:

> I believe that dance is the oldest, noblest and most cogent of the arts. I believe that dance is the most perfect symbol of the activity of God and His angels. I believe that dance has the power to heal, mentally and physically. I believe that true education in the art of dance is education of the whole man. . . .(Newsletter, Spring 1972, P.1.)

These words have inspired sacred dancers for many years, and the activities of the Sacred Dance Guild have given flesh and substance to these beliefs throughout its history. By 1974, the Guild was becoming more aware of itself as a potent ingredient in the religious art world and as a vanguard in liturgical development.

CHAPTER V

1975-1978

Two solid individuals mark this final period -- Martha Yates (President 1975-1977) and Doug Adams (President 1977-1979). Martha took the presidency at a time when the Guild was in a state of flux (it seems to have always been that way) with many new directions open to it. Her basic plan was to keep this "ship" on a steady course, and to take the time to study the history of the Guild. Martha said the Sacred Dance Guild must keep on an even keel and not jump into unknown untested waters. Her approach was very simple: take the time to solidify the Guild without making any radical changes. It takes discernment to know when _not_ to do something.

Organizationally speaking, the main issues remained: 1) the by-laws which _still_ needed tightening up, and 2) the expansion of regions (which depended on number one). In one way the situation looked rather pathetic -- that a twenty year old organization was still trying to set its legal base at a painfully slow pace; and that a ten year old plan for regionalization was still being discussed, again with very slow progress. Not a very good track record! It could discourage one from having any hope in the Sacred Dance Guild's future at all. And, indeed, at least in part, it could account for the lagging membership. The Sacred Dance Guild does not have a commendable history of good, solid, progressive organization -- that is obvious from the evidence. There have been many fine leaders with optimistic dreams but they have completed their terms with a feeling of weight and lack of movement -- a very bad feeling for dancers! For such a small organization the weight of it and the inertia has been all out of proportion to its size. And the reason was basically that lack of a firm foundation on which to grow.

That is why these two leaders, Martha and Doug, have been crucial to the Sacred Dance Guild. Quite intentionally, Martha Yates "marked time" to give the Guild that opportunity to take stock of itself, to uncover its history, and to build a sense of fellowship and community among the leaders and members at large. In her loving way, Martha affirmed her co-workers through letters and meetings and encouraged and challenged the membership through the Newsletter. Before one can dance one must learn to breathe and become attuned to one's body. Just so, Martha felt, the Guild must take time to breathe and to become attuned to its body -- all the members.

Doug Adams has been able to utilize this quiet period (I am using the word quiet only at the organizational level -- as the reader will see, the membership of the Guild has been very busy and growth at the grass roots has been very strong.), and with his power house energy took the presidency in June of 1977 with the goal of "Building a floor under Sacred Dance". The time has come to make the foundation sure, and Doug has supplied the strong, dynamic leadership to do just that. He is a professor of Worship and the Arts at the Pacific School of Religion in Berkeley, California and on the doctoral Faculty in "theology and dance" at Graduate Theological Union and fortunately is mobile enough to travel around the country on different speaking and workshop engagements -- an asset the Guild is enjoying for the first time in its President.

The "floor" that Doug has pledged to build is basically a financial base with theological dimensions. In his first article as President in the Fall 1977 Newsletter, titled, "Ask and

You Shall Receive, Knock and it Shall be Opened", he encouraged members to give to the Margaret Taylor Endowment for Dance at the Pacific School of Religion which was designated for Sacred Dance giving during 1977-79. (See Appendix VII.) Said Doug:

> We are at a crucial time for developing Sacred Dance. There is enormous interest among students in seminaries as well as many lay persons. Will we provide the courses and workshops on sacred dance at seminaries to develop such interest in the future leaders of churches? I firmly believe that the future of sacred dance depends upon our response to that question. (Newsletter, Fall 1977, p. 17.)

In his second article, "Building a Floor Under Sacred Dance", Doug spoke of two places to concentrate financial resources to help promote the cause of sacred dance. One was the Margaret Taylor Endowment and the other was the National Sacred Dance Guild Endowment which provides scholarships for those who need help to attend the annual Sacred Dance Institute. (This fund had originally been called the Ruby Henderson Memorial, then the Virginia Lucke Memorial.) Doug regards these two funds as very important investments in the future leaders in sacred dance. In fact, these two funds could be somewhat of an indicator of the health of sacred dance. Without strong financial bases the Guild cannot grow to the heights it should.

Besides his interest in the financial base of the Sacred Dance Guild, Doug has also been encouraging a sound theological foundation for sacred dance. He requested that Judy Rock, an ordained minister as well as an outstanding dancer from California who also teaches sacred dance at Pacific School of Religion, write an article for the _Newsletter_. In response to his request, Judy submitted an essay titled, "Liturgical Dance as Theology". These are some of her piercing thoughts:

> Anything which is done as part of a worship service is, by definition, a theological expression: an expression of the relationship of a person or a community to God. Liturgical dance . . .is . . . a kind of kinesthetic theology. The theological image is presented through the body. This means that liturgical dance, whether performed dance or congregational movement, must be both good dance and good theology.
> . . . In other words, liturgical dance must first be good dance -- i.e., skillfully performed . . . and capable of communicating through the movement the theological image in question -- in order to be good theology. (_Newsletter_, Fall 1977, p. 29.)

Thus Judy added a new dimension to the age-long debate of skilled dancer vs. spiritual depth -- that of the relationship between form and content: dance skill and theological image. They cannot be separated. But, as Judy said:

> It is all too possible to have good dance which is _not_ good theology. . . . Any particular liturgical dance is the form given at a particular point in time to some part of this theological content. . . . To put it very simply . . . what do you believe? (_Newsletter_, Fall 1977, p. 29.)

Judy has challenged, therefore, not only the form (technical skill), but also the content (theological image). She has seen some very good dances with very bad theology:

> I have seen several profoundly moving and shaking religious dances. But if I had to judge on the basis of most of the dances I have seen, I could only conclude that those several dances were oddities -- perhaps even heresies! . . . I would wonder if anyone ever got passionate about Christianity. . . .I would be convinced that Christians have no pelvises. . . . I would assume that the Christian life is a rather tepid, bland way, in which the supreme goal is to be happy and nice. . . . that the chief Christian virtue is everyone doing the same thing at the same time. I would have no idea that there had ever been such passionate, crazy, and wonderful people as saints; no conception of what could inspire people to build cathedrals or allow themselves to be beaten up in Selma,

> Alabama; no possible way to begin to experience the terror and delight and comfort of Emmanuel, God-With-Us. And this would be a tragedy in relation to a tradition whose center is Incarnation -- the Word made Flesh! (Newsletter, Fall 1977, p. 29-30.)

These are bold words! Judy has challenged her reader to think through his or her beliefs -- to discover the fulness of God and His activity -- the ironies and contradictions in our relationships with each other and with God, and then, to incorporate these facets of the theological content into skillful dance. Judy's contribution to the 'floor' of Sacred Dance is a strong and vital theological statement.* Hopefully, many will build on that 'floor'.

As that financial and theological foundation is laid, there is a hint in the air that

---

* Judy Rock expanded this statement in her booklet, Theology In the Shape of Dance, (Austin: The Sharing Company, 1978). Doug Adams has explored the interrelations of dance and theology in his book Congregational Dancing In Christian Worship and more recently in Dancing Christmas Carols. He and Judy Rock are currently teaching courses together at Pacific School of Religion on Dance as a Shape of Theology and project a publication entitled Criteria In Christian Dance.

the identity of the Guild is about to solidify. As has been stated many times in this paper, the identity has been very hazy with changing, unclear shapes throughout its history. A poignant illustration of that lack of clarity is the absence of a symbol for the Sacred Dance Guild. In May 1976, a logo pin committee was organized. (Minutes, May 1976.) Through the Newsletter, members were invited to create a symbol which would most closely encapsule the image of the Sacred Dance Guild. The response was sparse. The suggestions that did come in were rejected. As yet, there is no logo. This is a very significant facet in the profile of the Guild. The desire for the logo reveals that search for a tangible identity. But, as yet, no one has quite precisely made that image clear.

But, whoever the Guild is, there are definite signs of growth and some of those signs are more than indicators -- they are directional for the future. In June of 1975, new regions were established with directors: southeast, upper south, south central, central pacific and inter-mountain. These areas had shown for many years that they were growing in membership and were capable of sustaining high quality leadership. And the establishment of new regional directors even in areas with few members stimulated the spectacular growth of the Guild from 1975-1978. (See Appendix V.) Colorado, especially, has been a vanguard in setting up quasi-independent regional areas. Connie Fisher of Denver had sent in a report in 1969, which was quoted in the last chapter, about how busy sacred dance was in this area. In the Fall 1975 Newsletter, items from Colorado covered four and a half pages, and in the Winter 1976-77 Newsletter, they used over six pages to report their exciting news. They formed themselves into the Rocky Mountain Sacred Dance Guild complete with officers, Newsletter, periodic workshops and official logo! And that Regional Guild has some fifty members at the regional level. Connie Fisher has been the main inspiration for this development. She stated:

> Sacred dance has grown steadily in the Rocky Mountain states. . . . there are ten national SDG members in Colorado, one in Utah, and three in Montana, three of those being group memberships. . . . Most of these members were encouraged to join the Sacred Dance Guild by myself or the local group in Denver. . . . The local guild also has a Newsletter which ties the groups together between events and workshops. Members are urged to join the Sacred Dance Guild national. . . . There are three meetings a year in addition to workshops. . . .
> I would like to add a word as to the importance of local groups, which are

> affiliated with the Sacred Dance Guild. When the Guild was first organized, it was an important support group to the work of sacred dance in the Eastern States, for that is where most of the work was going on. . . . But . . . I have worked almost always alone. The cost was prohibitive to attend the Institutes, which were always two to three thousand miles away. The local group here in Denver has done a great deal to encourage and instruct new leaders of sacred dance. . . . It is hoped that more National Workshops will be held in the Midwest or West. (Newsletter, Fall 1976-77, p. 19.)

This request to have the Sacred Dance Guild hold national workshops in the western states was probably the most blatant and most reasonable ever stated on this particular issue. Connie's description of their very responsible and creative activities in Colorado made it a completely valid suggestion. In fact, it was hinted that the health and vision of the Guild depended on an unqualified affirmative response. More and more people like Connie could see that the growth of the Guild depended on responsibly organized regional development. But, Connie added the need for the Sacred Dance Guild to be officially represented with national workshops in other parts of the country than the Northeast.

Pennsylvania has been another area, though

it had a slow start in the sixties, that has been growing rapidly and is getting organized, thanks to the persistent efforts of Alice Rader. In the Fall of 1976, Alice announced a:

> "Build the Guild Project" . . . toward a stronger foundation and framework. Please send me ideas you may have for development of regions. I am beginning to collect material for a purposeful resource notebook to lend support and direction to the position of Regional Publicity Directors. (Newsletter, Fall 1976-77, p. 19.)

Alice has been faithfully in contact with the members of her area and has organized several workshops. She is keenly aware of the importance of her official position and is demonstrating valuable leadership in developing the creative possibilities of the position of Regional Publicity Director.

Other areas, too, have begun to blossom. Aldema Ridge of Columbia, Maryland reported continued growth in the Upper South Region, with the help of a workshop led by Mary Jane Wolbers. Dorothy Johnson, Regional Director of that area, reported that:

In January (1977) a steering committee met to form a local Sacred Dance Guild chapter

> -- to encompass Richmond, Fredericksburg and areas within an easy distance of Washington. We are grateful to have information and encouragement from Connie Fisher -- the Rocky Mountain Sacred Dance Guild is a thriving model. (Newsletter, Winter 1976-77, p. 26.)

And in Portland, Oregon - Southwest Washington area, Susan Cole has drawn together over 30 persons into National Sacred Dance Guild membership, with periodic workshops featuring Doug Adams, Judy Rock, and Carla DeSola and regular local sharing sessions. Thus, the example begun in Denver, Colorado is beginning to have an impact on other areas that are aware of their own sense of growth and readiness for organization.

As different areas grow stronger and become organized, this also has an impact on the individual professional dancer. A few individuals, very few, have begun to see the possibilities of sufficient interest in sacred dance to support a dancer either full or part time. In 1973, for example, Robert Yohn was commissioned to choreograph "Trinity Mass" to a rock score. (Newsletter, Fall 1973, p.22.) And, in the Spring of 1976, Bob happily reported: "For the first time I think one could have a tour in sacred dance that would pay for itself." (Newsletter, Spring 1976-77, p. 11.)

He had just completed a tour in Colorado and California in twenty-three days, the results of which were very exciting, both for Bob and the people he visited. Cooperation between two strong Regional Sacred Dance Guilds made the tour possible as Colorado and California split the cost of Bob Yohn's travel costs and arranged many local classes and workshops. In 1978, Pacific School of Religion brought Carla DeSola to California allowing the Portland Guild to extend her tour to Oregon with little additional expense.

From Birmingham, Alabama, Suanne Ferguson actually gave up her job with the Birmingham Ballet, and is now "working full time for the church as Director of Movement Education for the kindergarten and Director of Leisure ministries." (Newsletter, Spring 1976-77, p. 21.) An interesting job title to say the least! This was the first entry in the history of the Guild of someone hired by a church to do sacred dance!

Nancy Brock, from Huntington, Long Island, is another example of someone financially supported in a sacred dance project. She did a "research project supported by a grant from the Board of College Education and Church Vocations of the Lutheran Church in America."

(Newsletter, Fall 1975-76, p. 331.) From that research she has developed a lecture-demonstration called "The Dance in Worship", which has been presented in churches, schools, and colleges since 1971. In her program, Nancy has included dances from different periods of history going back to primitive and ancient peoples, early Christians, part of a liturgical music drama of the twelfth century, and examples of Shaker dances. She has also utilized congregational dancing. In March, 1975, she was invited by the Analytical Psychology Club of New York to do her program under the title of "The Dance of Life: From the Demonic to the Sacred". She adapted her discussion to emphasize:

> . . .psychological aspects rather than the specific use of dance in church services, showing how dance is a potent force in healing, both physical and psychological, and a source of spiritual renewal leading toward wholeness in the individual and community in the group. (Newsletter, Fall 1975-76, p. 33-34.)

So, a project initially supported by a grant developed into a program which Nancy has been able to adapt to a number of situations and which she has shown around the New York area, down in Virginia, Maryland, Pennsylvania, and as far away as Kentucky. Nancy has shown that sacred dance responsibly and intelligently performed is a tremendous educational tool besides being a spiritual channel.

The long lists of activities of the members in the Newsletters of the last few years (compare two thirds of a page in 1960 with seventeen pages in 1977) have been a potent testimony to the growth of the Guild. And, not only do members send in a description of their dances and experiences. They have been reflecting and theologizing on them as well. What actually happens at the experiential and emotional level is being described in vivid detail that zeroes right in on the event. An illustration of this is a reflection by Mary Hynding from California who was dancing with the Reverend Jacqueline Meadows in a Maundy Thursday Service:

> The Last Supper. The night Christ turned over his kingship to the twelve, and they were told to turn it over to all people. The night Judas realized he was about to betray Christ. The night Christ changed the meaning of passover. My body, my blood. . . . do this in remembrance of me. The night there was pain all around the table. Judas' agony, sadness of losing a friend, Christ's terror at the prospect of being killed, his humaneness, his love, the fellowship of communion. The music lifts me out of the pew. You could say I'm waiting for a cue, but I am

> more aware of Christ in time. The sadness of the night, my mourning of someone loved and lost, not necessarily Christ, but he is mixed up in there too. I begin to move and Judas' agony grips me. The pain is real. Jacquie is moving toward me and I can tell her agony is real too. We start to interact -- pain on top of pain. Suddenly I am Jesus -- frightened, running, hiding behind the communion rail, tired, crying at the table over the sacraments. The hell of it! Suddenly Jacquie is drawing me out. Pulling. Not with her hands but with the energy of life, love, giving, hope. The hurt, the agony, the pain are real but there is communion -- a closeness of spirit. Maundy Thursday ends. (_Newsletter_, Spring 1974-75, p. 13.)

The intensity of emotion felt by Mary as she danced the part of Judas was not lost in technical performance or pre-arranged cues. For a time she actually embodied Judas and all the Judas's who have betrayed Christ. From the description, one can expect that the congregation, too, was swept into the intensity of the event through the power of this dance drama.

Another event, this one from Seattle, Washington, was described by Barja Nazaretiz from a similar emotional point of view. Even the choice of words indicate a feeling of electricity during the service:

> The entire service is a sea of movement

> exchange with extemporaneous activity. At this activity church, one is left breathless in that the entire congregation makes an effort to participate substantially in movement, singing, and worship. Dancing (extemporaneous) is a natural part of the service as is the contribution from the choir. (Newsletter, Fall 1975-76, p. 37.)

Actually, this quote is describing congregational dance, but it is interesting primarily as an illustration of the emotional results of movement -- either individual or group. Barja said that "one is left breathless" during the service, that one's emotional involvement is so strong. The earlier years of the Guild did not describe their sacred dance experiences in such a fashion. As Doug Adams has said, "Dance can enable the congregation to feel what it believes." (Newsletter, Winter 1976-77, p. 20.)

The importance of the emotional dimension was described by Nancy Brock of Long Island in an article in the Spring of 1977. It is unlikely that the early sixties would have accepted the notion of sacred dance as expressing emotional release. It was necessary that sacred dance become established in a "cooler" vein first. If it had been tagged "emotionalism", it would have hurt the sacred dance movement.

But people in the seventies are less afraid and suspicious of emotions and realize they are an integral, healthy part of the person. At any rate, Nancy had published an article, "The Ministry of Dance", in Friends General Conference Quarterly, Vo. 8, No. 4, Summer 1976, which was quoted in the Sacred Dance Guild Newsletter:

> Dance is a universal language. . . . But it is a symbolic language that defies translation into ordinary terms. It speaks not to the mind, but rather to that sixth sense, the kinesthetic, which causes us to respond to movement we observe with active, though invisible, participation of our own musculature. The dancer's message cannot be comprehended by the intellect; it speaks to the heart, not to the head. If it could be stated in words, there would be no need to dance it! . . .
> Feeling, not 'understanding', is the key.
> (Newsletter, Spring 1976-77, p. 9.)

Nancy's point is very clear: the key is "feeling" the dance, not "understanding" it.

Sufi dance, which has already been described, is based on the freeing of the mind and the emotions in preparation for the meditative state. There are some who have adapted the sufi style to the Judeo-Christian heritage. Vira Klawe of Long Island uses only

Hebrew and Christian terms in her songs to which she dances. Vira could see that unique ability of sufi dance to involve the dancers at a deep level and adapted it to her own very specific heritage.

The seventies have seen a renewal going on in the church which crosses all denominations. Sometimes called the charismatic movement (although the wide use of the term makes it difficult to peg a definition), it emphasizes the role of the Holy Spirit in daily lives and in the worship service, allowing for an emotional expression of one's devotion to God. Several members of the Sacred Dance Guild have been involved at some level in this renewal movement. Carla DeSola of New York said that sacred dance was really catching on right now particularly "among charismatics who enjoy freedom of emotion and physical expression." (Newsletter, Winter 1976-77, p. 6.) At the Baltimore General Charismatic Conference, Lori Jackson from the Lamb of God Community in Lutherville, Maryland danced with a group at a coffee house held during the conference. (Newsletter, Winter 1976-77, p. 25.) In Los Angeles, California, the Celebration Dancers directed by Antoinette Marie Scinocca joined a charismatic group in which they do much scriptural interpretation accompanied only be the reader's voice. (Newsletter, Spring 1974-75, p. 13.) Sister Jane Theresa Culligan described a Prayer and Praise weekend at the House of Prayer, Convent Station in New Jersey in which there was a "dancing in the spirit" workshop:

> . . .resulting in powerful healings through the experience of expressing one's inner feelings in relationship to God, through the body. Saturday evening a 'Freedom in Movement' workshop was offered increasing the ability to 'dance in the spirit'. At Mass on Sunday there was congregational participation in worshipping God through dance at the offertory, after Communion and also at the closing. A new depth of freedom was experienced by all who participated in this weekend of Praising the Lord. (Newsletter, Fall 1975-76, p. 33.)

Sister Jane's choice of words and description of the worship experience would be quite familiar to people involved in the charismatic movement.

The sense of being guided by the Holy Spirit has pervaded the experience of sacred dancers since the early years, but with the theological development in the church and with the spread of renewal and the charismatic movement, members have been more vocal about it and considerably more confident. The Oasis Ensemble of Boulder, Colorado, directed by Barbara Eller, described itself this way:

> A Christian group, the ensemble is a free lance, non-denominational, inter-religious, Spirit-filled, always changing, ever constant, alive organism which sees liturgy as the focal point around which life develops. (Newsletter, Fall 1975-56, p. 24.)

Similarly, the Sacred Dance Group of Boulder, Colorado revealed that same charismatic character in the description of its activities. Observe the language, enthusiasm and energetic optimism:

> Praise the Lord! . . . How we delight in and welcome the opportunity to share with our many brothers and sisters in the Lord's dance!
> The Sacred Dance Group of Boulder was formed in 1969 by Paula Douthett, under the inspiration of the Holy Spirit. The group since that time, under the Lord's principle of increase and multiplication has grown and flourished and multiplied into four groups with a fifth in the birth process. (Newsletter, Fall 1975-76, p. 27.)

The conviction that they are called by God to form these groups and to dance is felt by all their dancers. People come from different parts of Canada, United States, and England, as called by God to study in their "New School of Creative Dance and Ballet". Thus, the good news is shared around far parts of the world as these dancers return to their homes. The total object of all this activity is to help people to worship God more completely: "How wonderful it was to see multitudes lifting up their hands and arms and faces unto the Lord in praise and worship." (Newsletter, Fall 1975-76, p. 27.) One senses in their words that we are living in a special age: "In this day, we are seeing God restoring the arts to show forth his glory and truth. . . ." (Newsletter, Fall 1975-76, p. 27.) This force is an extremely potent one in the Sacred Dance Guild today.

And to see dance appearing in many special services which at one time were very conservative is becoming more and more common. Judy Rock of California danced at her husband's ordination and installation. (Newsletter, Winter 1976-77, p. 17.) The Salem Sacred Dance Group in Rochester, N.Y. under the direction of Evelyn Broadbent participated in the ordination service of Virginia Mackey. (Newsletter, Fall 1975-76, p. 33.) A young lay person is hoping, against a very conservative block, that sacred dance will be used in conjunction with adult immersionist Baptism such as is used in the Disciples of Christ and Baptist Churches. (Newsletter, Fall 1975-76, p. 19.) Berneice Fickes of Lancaster, Pennsylvania told of plans to dance the feet washing as recorded in the Gospel of John during the Maundy Thursday service. (Newsletter, Spring 1976-77, p. 26.) In a Memorial Service held at the June Institute of 1974 at Kirkridge, Pennsylvania, Guild members danced in tribute to Virginia Lucke. There is probably not an occasion left that has not been celebrated with dance -- wedding, baptism, death, ordination, Christmas, Easter, Thanksgiving.

And now no one is excluded from the dance -- the congregation, the halt and the lame and the blind: "We witness our faith through dance movement and expression. We work with the aged in wheelchairs, walkers and canes, presenting exercises for body, mind and spirit, sitting down." (Newsletter, Spring 1976-77, p. 16. Delhi Sacred Dancers, Modesto, Ca.) Everyone can dance. The Warren United Sacred Dance Choir, Denver, Colorado, has a mentally retarded member in their group who even wrote poetry to which the group danced. Everyone can dance. As Doug Adams so aptly stated:

> Each person has a skill to offer in dance worship: some to lead the congregational movement, some to dance solos, some to dance in choirs, some simply to sing along and move in folk patterns of movement. (*Newsletter*, Fall 1975-76, p. 9.)

Worship liturgy literally means the work of the people -- it can no longer be only a vicarious experience. In some way, all can be involved and today that includes dance.

CHAPTER VI

CONCLUSION

The Sacred Dance Guild of 1978 exhibits several varieties of dance among its members. It would be appropriate to conclude this history with a brief sketch of the seven main streams that I see running through the Guild. They exist harmoniously with one another and challenge us to broaden our concepts of that which constitutes sacred dance.

First, there is the sacred dance choir or soloist for whom the Guild was first formed, as was written into the "Purpose" in 1958. These are the people who, much like church singing choirs, rehearse regularly to prepare for a dance in the Sunday morning worship service or special program. Very often they dance during services that highlight the church year, e.g. Christmas, Easter, Thanksgiving, etc., although many choirs are not limited by the special seasons.

Second, there is the dance spectacular, that which is done more at a performance level like the religious drama, and very often by professional dancers who seek to convey their faith through the dance. The technical skills required here would generally surpass that of the average member of a sacred dance choir.

Third, <u>dance therapy</u> has found a highly respected position within the Guild. An increasingly exciting field which is developing rapidly in the dance world at large, it is a natural outlet for any dancer with a concern for healing and wholeness. The experiences within this stream are not intended for an audience, but require active, sensitive participation by all those involved. Dance therapy has proven valuable for people with physical afflictions ranging from the deaf, blind, and lame to less major problems, and for those with psychological handicaps, again ranging from very deep problems to the less traumatic. The American Dance Therapy Association with whom the Guild has a good relationship holds high standards for those who want to pursue this field at a professional level.

Fourth, <u>congregational dance</u> is flourishing in an age when audiences (and congregations) are desirous of participation. Just as the whole congregation sings hymns during the service, so now they are dancing. The movements are often folk-like steps or simple arm movements that anyone can do in the pew, or, if there is space and freedom, in the aisles and around the communion table.

Fifth, ethnic dance which has received ample attention through the years at Workshops (see Appendix IV) and sufi dance with its emphasis on union with the divine and group meditation through movement and song have made their particular impact on the Guild. As in congregational dance, most of these dances invite participation.

Sixth, in conjunction with a phenomenon in the Church known as the "charismatic movement", dance is finding a very special place. In prayer and praise meetings, dance is used to interpret Scripture and to accompany many of the "Spiritual Songs". The dances are either spontaneous in which a few or all join in, or they are rehearsed by a group and presented to the others as a gift to be "shared". The emphasis is less on performance and more on the response to the Holy Spirit as the giver of gifts.

And, seventh, though it receives little attention because of course it is not done publicly, it is the dance as private prayer. Movement complements words as the vehicle of prayer expressing praise or confession, supplication or surrender. Spontaneous movement by one who seeks communion with God can flow from violent turbulence to a restful quiet. On the other hand, slow comfortable gestures might become full risk-taking movements as God challenges one to a prophetic ministry. Tears of joy or repentence may follow the prayer as the dancer yields a body willing to be transformed to the God who is willing to reveal. Movement before God is at the same time a tremendously courageous and humbling offering. One becomes vulnerable before a God who seeks such for His Kingdom -- people willing to be molded as clay in His hands.

I do not presume that these seven streams describe all the activities of Guild members. A lot of work is being done with dance in the field of religious education and at summer camps in a relaxed fun-filled atmosphere. Improvisational dance by individuals and groups done for their own mutual joy has uplifted many spirits to experiences of worship and community. Experimentation with dance as part of multi-media presentations has been very successful. The list of various creative and imaginative works of members is long; and it grows constantly.

At the present time the Sacred Dance Guild is capable of holding and nurturing all of the many expressions of dance among its members. There is an increasing sense of togetherness and direction within the leadership and a growing sense of identity and pride among the members at large -- contributing significantly to a sure foundation. From a fairly narrowly defined position on sacred dance, i.e., dance presented by sacred dance choirs in a worship service, the Guild has developed a fuller, broader understanding which incorporates the varieties which have just been described. The many activities simply cannot be totally contained in neat categories. But that is good. It means the Guild is being challenged by expressions that defy positive definition. Thus, the Sacred Dance Guild must hold in tension the need to declare who it is with the risk of leaving certain elements undefined -- i.e., identity without parochialism.

The outline of this history has basically followed the ups and downs of the events within the super-structure of the Guild. The organization has been weak, despite a full line of excellent, capable leaders. But greater solidarity is being achieved through re-examining the possibilities of regionalization, firming up the By-Laws, and attempting to build a good financial base. However, I hope it is clear that the members themselves have had a large part in directing the history of the Guild. The activities at the grass roots level have always indicated the true identity of the Sacred Dance Guild. The face of the Guild today is indeed a reflection, not merely of a few in leadership positions, but of the vibrant, relentless, energetic people who name themselves as members.

Twenty years after its inception, the Sacred Dance Guild looks back on a rocky path filled with the proverbial choking weeds. But it is a path which has been well danced upon in many different ways. Jesus said to his disciples, "Be glad and dance for joy." (Luke 6:23, NEB) And we have danced. Not always experiencing victory, we have learned to bring our varied selves before Him in dance. While today we dance but dimly, we anticipate that Great Day when, face to face, all will be dances of joy.

EPILOGUE

REFLECTIONS FOLLOWING THE 1978 SDG FESTIVAL

In June of 1978, the Sacred Dance Guild celebrated its twentieth birthday at the Annual Sacred Dance Guild Festival. (Formerly called "Institute", "Festival" was chosen as a more appropriate title.) And indeed it was a celebration! -- five exciting days of activities, sharing, and teaching.

A well varied selection of leaders brought their particular gifts to a gathering of over one hundred twenty eager students of sacred dance. Carla de Sola, well known for her direction of the Omega Liturgical Dancers at St. John the Divine Cathedral in New York, and as author of Learning Through Dance and The Spirit Moves, was our prime leader in dance. Graced with quietly sensitive qualities and strong convictions, she persistently drew our attention to our Lord. We were guided to see how, through the offering of our dance, the Presence of God was opened to us.

"Brother Blue" introduced Festival members to an unusual dramatic form of story telling following the theme of the "butterfly" within us struggling to be free. His rhythmically chanting stories elicited strong response from all of us.

Sister Vincent de Paul, architect and artist, shared with us the fruits of her majestic work at the Sisters of Notre Dame Chapel. We had the immense privilege there of spending a day of workshops with Carla and of celebrating the Medieval Catholic Mass on Sunday morning.

The Calliope Consort, a group of five women specializing in music from Biblical times through the seventeenth century, played for us many of their pieces, describing the historical background of each. On Sunday morning their beautiful Medieval sounds provided the music for the Worship Service.

Besides these major leaders, Doug Adams led a session on dancing Christmas Carols. Six members of the Guild taught smaller classes: Sylvia Bryant, Carlynn Reed, Robert Yohn, Judith Rock, Linda Kahn Seaton, and Susan Gunn. These people provided the opportunity in smaller group situations for developing dances which became part of the Liturgy for Sunday.

Judging by the positive energy throughout

the Festival and the stack of letters which have found their way to the mail box of the Program Director, the Festival was an overwhelming success.

Having given the reader a thumbnail sketch of the Festival (detailed information and evaluation are recorded in the Fall 1978 Newsletter), I would like to point out four significant facets of the Anniversary celebration and conclude with what I consider to be a major issue which the Guild will soon have to face.

1. The attendance reached a record of over one hundred twenty. A gradual increase over the past number of years has presented a challenge to the Program Director in facilitating the learning experience of so many.

2. By means of a mail ballot in the Spring, an amendment to the By-Laws was approved making the legality of chapter formation an accomplished fact. (See Chapter III for the original proposal made in 1968.) At the Festival there was much discussion concerning the Amendment, and the Rocky Mountain Sacred Dance Guild submitted several statements clarifying details on the setting up of the chapters and the responsibilities to the National Guild. These were accepted at the Annual Meeting. Both Colorado and Pennsylvania

are major forerunners of Chapter Formation and are important models for the rest of the Guild.

3. The question of the virtual monopoly of the East in hosting the Annual Festivals was seriously considered. At the Annual Meeting, it was voted to approve two Festivals in 1980, to be held in Boston and Denver at non-conflicting times. The intention is to inaugurate a new tradition once the ramifications of such a practice are fully studied and the necessary By-Law accomodations made.

4. For the first time, prayer services representing specific religious traditions were held, this year from the Lutheran and United Church of Christ Churches. A third service, entitled "non-denominational" was intentionally more spontaneous and experimental. (These were in addition to the Catholic Mass.) The leaders of all three services had been selected well in advance of the Festival and detailed preparations had been made. The services, complete with dance offerings, were held at various times throughout the first few days.

As Doug Adams noted we are moving from the axial to the locomotor; we have moved beyond preoccupation with older problems and face the new. These four major accomplishments indicate a Guild which is growing and changing. However, the fourth one poses a dilemma for the future.

The Institutes in the past have always attempted to meet both the spiritual and liturgical needs of the participants. It was customary to draw together the dances choreographed in the workshops as a liturgical offering during the closing worship service. However, too often the dances gave more the appearance of "show and tell" rather than being an enabler of worship. Furthermore, liturgical traditions were generally ignored in the design of the service.

The various Prayer Services and the concluding Catholic Mass at this year's Festival were a serious attempt to deepen and enrich the spiritual quality of the gathering. For instance, it was felt by the Board of Directors that the Festival should culminate in a truly grand act of worship which would exhibit the strength of a liturgical structure from a particular ecclesiastical tradition. The Roman Catholic Mass celebrated by "Skip" Conlin was chosen for 1978.

Although such a shift to the use of specific liturgical traditions may not at first glance appear to be a radical move, there are indeed long range ramifications. To be specific, as a Guild we are an inter-faith organization spanning not only all Christian traditions but other religions as well. With such a broad spectrum of religious belief, how can we be effectively united in a worship experience that satisfies all and offends none?

It is increasingly evident to me that within the historic debate over the relationship between "sacred" and "dance" it is in the incongruities of the "sacred" with which the Guild will have to deal in the near future. The move this year to provide worship opportunities for specific traditions is both symptomatic of the need and a first step to meet it.

But, if we probe deeper into the religious spectrum within the Guild, it is not difficult to see that the major problem will not emerge within the Christian denominations who share a common confession but in the encounter with other religions as we gather in worship, a moment that calls forth the integrity of our faith and belief. It must be recognized that there are many for whom this makes no significant alteration in their worship, who freely interpret words, concepts, and prayers into their own theology. But there is a substantial number for whom this would constitute a breach of integrity. The stumbling block will be the need for a common understanding of the Object of worship, not simply the diversity of liturgical forms. For the majority of Christians the question will be: Is God as revealed as Father, Son, and Holy Spirit the One to whom our praise is given? When the year arrives to give equal time to a Unitarian Service or Islamic or Buddhist, how will the dilemma be resolved?

In essence, how can we most honestly express who we say we are? I am convinced that here lies the heart of the identity crisis of the Sacred Dance Guild mentioned several times in this history. We are a _religious_ organization, and we are a _dance_ organization. But which of these provides our solidarity when we come together? We are united completely within the various styles of dance. But we are united at the sacred level in only the most general and diffused way. Let me give an example. At the 1977 Guild Institute, a segment of the members absented themselves from what they considered to be an eclectic worship service on Sunday morning. Their Christian identity lived at home was jarred by the nebulous identity they were asked to assume that day. Also, it has been observed that our vague religious stance is a deterrent to some who otherwise might wish to join.

We are living in an age of increasing conviction and specificity in matters of faith. It should be no surprise that the Guild has been and will continue to be influenced by the religious mood of the times. We cannot pretend to be unified in faith when there are very real and basic differences. Can people of different faiths worship together in a meaningful way? If so, how? If not, what will be the identity of the Guild in the future?

The 1978 Festival celebrated a twenty-year history full of struggles, successes, and failures. As we close one chapter, another is boldly opened. We anticipate a Guild in the future strong enough to explore the new directions necessary to continue to build a community fashioned to glorify God and fitted to serve the needs of the faithful.

APPENDIX I

By-Laws

The Sacred Dance Guild

(as of June 30, 1978)

Article I - Name

The name of this orgainization shall be the SACRED DANCE GUILD.

Article II - Purpose

The purpose of this Guild shall be to stimulate interest in the dance as a religious art form and to provide a means of communication and training for dance choirs.

Article III - Membership

Membership shall be open to all who are interested in this field.

Article IV - Dues

Membership dues are paid on an annual or two-year basis. The dues cannot be changed without membership voting by ballot and finalized at the annual meeting. Membership and dues shall apply to regular, student, sponsors or group.

Article V - Officers

The officers shall be a President, Vice President, a Recording Secretary, a Corresponding Secretary, a Treasurer, Membership Director, Newsletter Editor, National Program Director, National Publicity Director, Helps and Guidelines Director, National Director of Regions, Financial Advisor, and nine Directors.

Article VI - Executive Board

The executive board shall consist of the Officers named in Article V and Directors of Standing Committees.

Article VII-Duties of Officers

Section 1. The president shall preside at all meetings of the Guild and of the Executive Board. In the event of a vacancy on the Board, the President shall appoint a replacement until the annual meeting.

Section 2. The Vice President shall supplement the President and shall preside in the absence of the President.

Section 3. The Recording Secretary shall keep a record of each meeting and prepare a report for the Executive Board members.

Section 4. The Corresponding Secretary shall notify members of the time and place of meetings, keep a record of applications for membership, and answer all correspondence, and shall be responsible for keeping the mailing list up to date and for furnishing copies of it to Publicity Director and, upon request, to committees responsible for publicizing Guild functions.

Section 5. The Treasurer shall receive, hold, and pay out the funds, shall keep an itemized account of all receipts, appropriations, and expenditures, and shall submit a statement of finances at the meetings.

Section 6. The Financial Advisor shall be the immediate past Treasurer and shall help orient and advise the incumbent Treasurer.

Article VIII - Meetings

There shall be one general meeting a year known

as the Annual Meeting and Workshop and at least three executive board meetings a year to carry on activities of the Guild.

Article IX - Elections

Section 1. Elections shall be by ballot at the annual meeting and by proxy vote. Officers shall be elected to serve for one year. Three Directors shall be elected annually to serve for three years. (Note Article V-Officers. Nine Directors in all, three retiring, six remaining, three taking office each year.)

Section 2. The nominating committee will present a slate of officers mailed out prior to the annual meeting and returned by the beginning of the annual meeting.

Article X - Committees

Section 1. The President shall appoint a nominating committee of three members. This committee shall nominate a list of Officers, a Director of Membership, a Director of National Publicity, Directors of Regional Publicity, Newsletter Editor, Helps and Guidelines Director, National Program Director, National Director of Regions, Financial Advisor, Sacred Dance Guild Memorial Endowment Director.

Section 2. The Nominating Committee shall be a rotating one, one member to retire after serving three years (the third year as Chairman), the second member moving up to Chairman for the next year, and the third, new member being appointed each year by the President.

Section 3. The Nominating Committee Chairman must mail slate one month in advance to the Newsletter Editor prior to the annual meeting so the membership may cast their ballot by mail prior to the annual meeting.

Section 4. The Membership Director shall receive dues, send out membership cards, give the names of new members to the Recording Secretary, the Corresponding Secretary, and to the President, and give money and names to the Treasurer; also shall prepare mailing labels for the Newsletter Editor.

Section 5. a. To groups and media outside the Sacred Dance Guild, the National Publicity Director shall publicize national and regional Sacred Dance Guild activities and seek cooperation with other groups to enhance SDG purposes.

b. The National Director of Regions shall assist regional directors to plan workshops, have advance notices and post write-ups of these and other regional activities sent to the Newsletter Editor, and shall aid the creation of new chapters.

Section 6. a. With the advice and cooperation of the Board of Directors of the Sacred Dance Guild, the President shall appoint one committee member each year for a three year term on the Memorial Endowment Scholarship Fund.

b. The President will also fill any vacancies which occur mid-term in this committee.

c. Committee members may be reappointed any number of times.

Section 7. The National Program Director shall act as coordinator of all Guild program activities, may assist Directors in appointing committees for workshops, and other functions, assist these committees in the planning of same, and keep a complete record of all Guild sponsored events.

Section 8. The Newsletter Editor prepares, edits, prints, assembles and mails the Newsletter at least three times a year.

Section 9. The Helps and Guidelines Director gathers, assembles, and mails the Sacred Dance Guild Kit, and prepares the same for reprints and additions.

Article XI - Regional Chapters

Section 1. To further the purposes of the Sacred Dance Guild, chapters of the Sacred Dance Guild may be formed at regional, state, or local levels.

Section 2. To initiate a chapter, at least 15 members of the Sacred Dance Guild (who live within the proposed chapter area) shall sign a petition to the Sacred Dance Guild president requesting that the chapter be recognized.

Section 3. The petition to the president will include the proposed by-laws of the chapter and the projected budget and programs for the chapter.

Section 4. The Sacred Dance Guild president shall circulate such a petition to the Executive Board. Upon the affirmative vote of the majority of those Executive Board members voting, the chapter will be established according to the terms set forth in the chapter's by-laws, projected budget and program.

Section 5. Each chapter will nominate the person to serve on the Executive Board as regional director from that chapter's region. (Regional directors from regions without chapters shall continue to be nominated as noted in Article X, Section 5.)

Section 6. Changes in the chapter's by-laws will require the same procedure as that used to initiate and establish chapters. (See sections 2, 3, and 4 of this article.

Article XII - Amendments

The By-Laws may be amended by a two-thirds vote of the members present or represented by proxy in writing and voting at the Annual Meeting, provided that the proposed amendment is included in the announced agenda for the meeting. Amendments shall be drawn up by the Executive Board and presented for discussion and vote at the general organization meeting.

APPENDIX II

SACRED DANCE GUILD ORGANIZATIONAL CHART FEB. 1968

NATIONAL BOARD

President

3 Vice Pres.-Coord.
Geog. Areas

Rec. Secretary

Corres. Secretary

Treasurer
Memb. Chairman
Director Prog. Dev.
Nat. Publicity Chmn.
Pub. Rel. Chairman
Publications Editor

Newsletter Editor

Directors:

Chairmen from each
Region

Vice President Eastern States	Vice President Middle States	Vice President Western States
E. Regional Chapters Numbers Unlimited	Mid.Regional Chapters Numbers Unlimited	West. Regional Chapters Numbers Unlimited

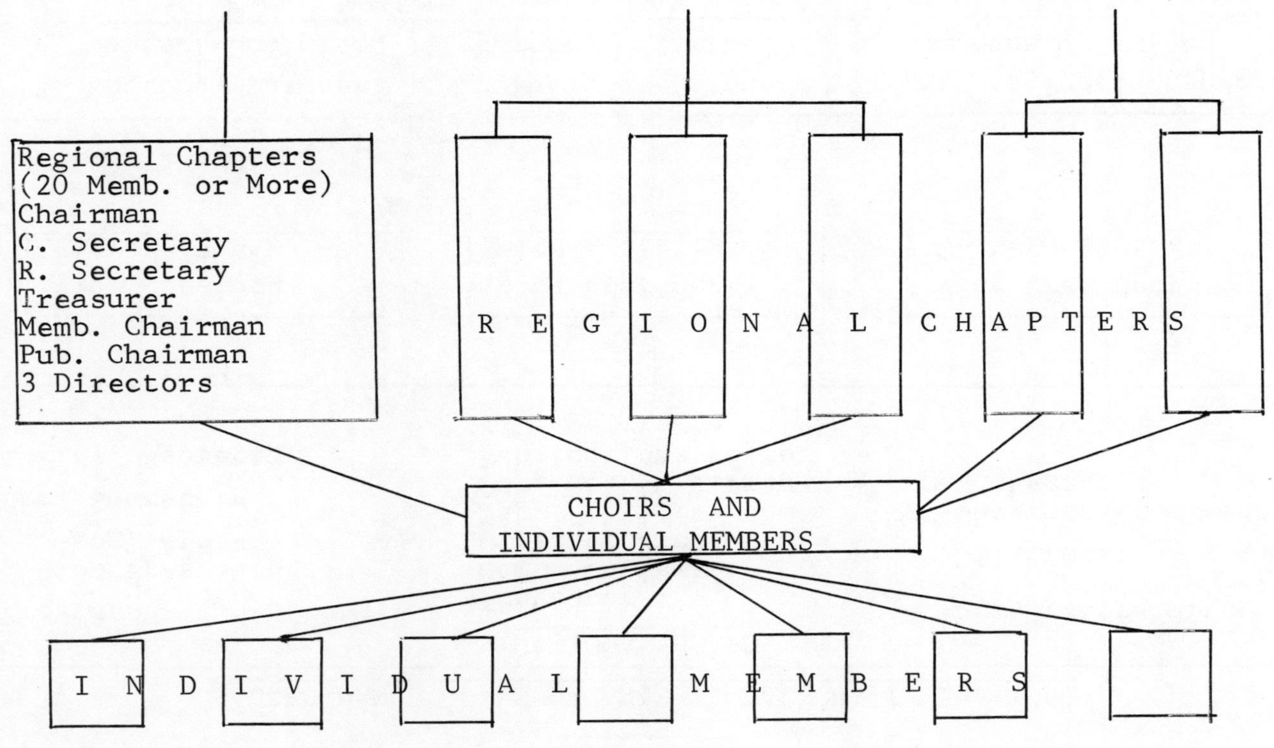
Regional Chapters
(20 Memb. or More)
Chairman
C. Secretary
R. Secretary
Treasurer
Memb. Chairman
Pub. Chairman
3 Directors
REGIONAL CHAPTERS
CHOIRS AND INDIVIDUAL MEMBERS
INDIVIDUAL MEMBERS

APPENDIX III

OFFICERS OF SDG 1958-78

1958-59:

Pres.: Jane Renz
Vice: Avis-Ann Parke
Rec.Sec.: Beatrice Jenkins
C. Sec.: Thelma Atwood
Treas.: Josephine Rice
Pub.: Mary Jane Wolbers
Memb.: Helen Borngesser
Editors: Avis-Ann Parke
Mrs. D. B. Chamberlain
Mrs. N. Walz

1960:

Pres.: Mrs. Willis Rayton, Hanover, N.H.
Vice.: Mrs. Charles Wolbers, New Platz, N.Y.
R.Sec.: Miss Elsie Simmons, Providence, R.I.
C.Sec.: Mrs. David Chamberlain, Staten Is., N.Y.
Treas.: Mrs. Theo Rice, Melrose, MA
Memb.: Miss Hazel Bailey, Quincy, MA
Prog.: Rev. Robert Storer, Winchester, MA
Pub. : Mrs. Charles Wolbers
Editors: Mrs. Charles Wolbers
Mrs. Jeanne Saunders, Weston, MA
Miss Joyce Kydd, Fall River, MA
Directors:
Mr. J. Henderson, MA
Mrs. B. Borgesser, MA
Mrs. E. Renz, MA
Mrs. W. Taylor, Wash., D.C.
CT: Mrs. C. Simpson
ME,NH,VT: Rev. J. Buell
MA: Miss D. Creed
NJ: Miss R. Smith
NY: Mrs. C. Wolbers

1961:

Pres.: Ruth Rayton, Hanover, NH
Vice.: Mary Jane Wolbers, New Platz, NY
R.Sec.: Elizabeth Chenell, Concord, NH

C.Sec.: Janet Walz, Park Ridge, NJ
Treas.: Josephine Rice, Melrose Highland,NJ
Memb.: Miss Hazel Bailey, Quincy, MA
Prog.: Rev. Robert Storer, Winchester, MA
Pub.: Mary Jane Wolbers
Editors: Martha Odom, Springfield, MA
Lura Ellsworth, Branford, CT
Martha Frizzell, Charlestown, NH
Directors:
Mr. J. Henderson, MA
Mrs. B Borngesser, MA
Mrs. E. Renz, MA
Mrs. W. Taylor, Wash.,DC
Mrs. M. Herric, RI
Mrs. R. Hart, MT
CT: Mrs. C. Simpson
ME,NH,VT: Rev. J. Buell
MA: Miss D. Creed
NJ: Miss R. Smith
NY: Mrs. C. Wolbers

1962:

Pres.: Mary Jane Wolbers, New Platz, NY
Vice.: Rev. Robert Storer, Winchester, MA
R.Sec.: Elizabeth Chenelle, Falmouth, ME
C.Sec.: Janet Walz, Wharton, NJ
Treas.: Jeanne Saunders, Weston, MA
Prog.: Janet Knight, E. Longmeadow, NY
Memb.: Hazel Bailey, Quincy, MA
Pub.: Judy Bennett, Sloatsburg, NY
Editor: Margaret Fisk Taylor, Athens, OH
Directors:
Mr. S. Arendholz, MA
Mrs. W. Rayton, NH
Mrs. J. Radin, NJ
Mrs. M.F.Taylor, OH
Mrs. N. Andersen, MI
Mrs. R. Hart, MT
Mrs. R. Odom, MA
Mrs. C. Reynolds, PA
Mrs. H. D. Gray, CT
CT: Mrs. J. Lucke
ME,NH,VT: Mrs. J. Lepeschkin
MA: Mrs. J. Smith

NJ: Mrs. R. Schayer
NY: W. Porter
PA: Mrs. E. Renz
RI: Miss E. Simmons

1963:

Pres. Mary Jane Wolbers, New Platz, NY
Vice: Rev. Robert Storer, Winchester, MA
R.Sec.: Charlotte Wright, Fall River, MA
C.Sec.: Janet Walz, Wharton, NJ
Treas.: Jeanne Saunders, Weston, MA
Prog.: Jeanne Fuller, Darien, CT
Memb.: Hazel Bailey, Quincy, MA
Pub.: Judy Bennett, Sloatsburg, NY
Editor: Margaret Fisk Taylor, Athens, OH
Directors:
Mrs. J. Henderson, MA
Mrs. W. Rayton, NH
Mrs. J. Radin, NJ
Mrs. N. Andersen, MI
Mrs. J. Canino, NY
Mrs. R. Odom, MA
Mrs. R. Hart, MT
Mrs. T. Rice
Mrs. H. D. Gray, CT
CT: Mrs. J. Lucke
ME,NH,VT: Mrs. K. Duston
MA: Mrs. J. Smith
NJ: Mrs. R. Schayer
NY: W. Porter
PA: Mrs. E. Wagner
RI: Miss E. Simmons

1964:

Pres.: Mrs. W. Johnson, NH
Vice: Mrs. Robert Sonen, Orange, NJ
R.Sec.: Mrs. M. Webb Wright, Woodbury, CT
C.Sec.: Mrs. Coy L. Huffine, Winchester, MA
Treas.: Jeanne Saunders, Weston, MA
Memb.: Mrs. O. Sherwood, Yonkers, NY
Prog.: Jeanne Fuller, Darien, CT
Pub.: Judy Bennett, Sloatsburg, NY
Editor: Margaret Fisk Taylor, Athens, OH

Directors:
Mrs. J. Henderson, MA
Mrs. W. Rayton, NH
Mrs. C. Wolbers, PA
Mrs. N. Andersen, MI
Mrs. J. Canino, NY
Miss H. Bailey
Rev. R. Storer
Mrs. T. Rice
Mrs. H. D. Gray
CT: Mrs. C. Baxter
ME,NH,VT: Mrs. C. Broadbent
MA: Mrs. T. Rice
NJ: Mrs. R. Schayer
NY: W. Porter
PA: Mrs. E. Wagner
RI: Miss E. Simmons
S.East: Miss C. Trump
Midwest: Mrs. J. Lucke
Calif: Mrs. E. Roberts

1965:

Pres.: Mrs. Warren T. Johnson, Peterborogh, NH
Vice.: Mrs. Robert A. Sonen, Orange, NJ
R.Sec.: Mrs. M. Webb Wright, Woodbury, CT
C.Sec.: Mrs. Coy L. Huffine, Winchester, MA
Treas.: Mrs. N. M. Andersen, Saginaw, MI
Memb.: Mrs. Allen Hollis, Fall River, MA
Prog.: Mrs. Robert Sonen, Orange, NJ
Co-Chair: Mrs. H.D. Gray, Hartford, CT
Pub.: Miss Dorothy Creed, Milton, MA
Editor: Mrs. Walter Taylor, Athens, OH
Directors:
Mr. J. Henderson, MA
Mrs. C. Wolbers, PA
Mrs. J. Canino, NY
Miss H. Bailey, MA
Rev. R. Storer, MA
Mrs. T. Rice, MA
Mrs. P. Fuller, CT
Mrs. N. Saunders, MA
Mrs. O. Sherwood, NY
Calif: Mrs. E. Roberts
CT: Mrs. C. Baxter

ME,NH,VT:Mrs. C. Broadbent
MA: Mrs. T. Rice
NJ: Mrs. K. Jefferson
PA: Mrs. C. Reynolds
NY: M. Slier
Midwest:Mrs. J. Lucke
MI Mrs. M. Schlegel
S. East:M. C. Trump

1966:

Pres.: Mrs. Robert Sonen, W. Orange, NJ
Vice.: Mrs. Prescott Fuller, Darien, CT
R.Sec.: Mrs. E. H. Slier, N. Babylon, NY
C.Sec.: Mrs. Coy L. Huffine, Winchester, MA
Treas.: Mrs. Nels Andersen, Saginaw, MI
Memb.: Mrs. Orion Sherwood, Yonkers, NY
Prog.: Mrs. Naomi Aleh-Leaf, Swanpscott, MA
Co-Chair:Mrs. Henry Millonig, Kingston, NY
Pub.: Mrs. David Bennett, Cornwall, NY
Editor: Mrs. Walter A. Taylor, Athens, OH
Directors:
Mr. J. Henderson, MA
Mrs. J. Carruthers, NY
Rev. R. Storer, MA
Mrs. W. Johnson, NH
Mrs. C. Wolbers, PA
Rabbi M. Richman, PA
Mrs. N. Saunders, MA
Mrs. M. Wright, CT
Calif: Mrs. E. Roberts
CT: Mrs. C. Baxter
ME,NH,VT:Mrs. C. Broadbent
MA: Mrs. K. Sparrow
NJ: Mrs. K. Jefferson
PA: Mrs. D. Parke
NY: Mrs. D. Dexter
Midwest:Mrs. J. Lucke
Outreach:Mrs. W. Tucker

1967-1968:

Pres.: Mrs. Robert Sonen, NJ
Vice.: Mrs. Noami Aleh-Leaf, MA
R.Sec.: Mrs. E. H. Slier, NY

C.Sec.: Mrs. L. Intravaia, Carbondale, IL
Treas.: Mrs. Nels Andersen, **MI**
Memb.: Mrs. Orion Sherwood, NY
Co: Mrs. Carl Hartman, NY
Prog.: Mrs. John Lucke, Grand Rapids, MI
Pub.: Mrs. Henry Millonig, NY
Editor: Mrs. David Bennett, NY
Directors:
Mrs. C. Wolbers, PA
Rev. Mr. D. Miller, NJ
Mrs. I.Kanter, MA
Mrs. M. Wright, CT
Mrs. W. Johnson, MH
Rev. Mr. J. Miller, NJ
Mr. J. Henderson, MA
Rabbi M. Richman, PA
Mrs. M. Taylor, OH
Calif: Mrs. E. Roberts
CT: Mrs. F. Holden
ME,NH,VT:Mrs. C. Broadbent
MA: Mrs. K. Sparrow
NJ: Mrs. S. Jefferis
PA: Mrs. D. Parke
NY: Mrs. D. Dexter
Midwest: Mrs. H. Loomis
Outreach:Mrs. W. Tucker

<u>1969-1970</u>:

Pres.: Margaret Fisk Taylor, Oberlin, OH
Vice.: Noami Aleh-Leaf, MA
R.Sec.: Sister Grace, O.S.H.Convent,Vails G.,NY
C.Sec: Virginia Lucke, MI
Treas.: Toni Intravaia, IL
Memb.: Wendy Hartman, NY
Prog.: Rev. Daren Miller, Dunellen, NJ
Pub.: Marion DuBois, Newburgh, NY
Editor: Judith Bennett, NY
Directors:
Mrs. C. Wolbers, PA
Mrs. I. Kanter, MA
Mrs. C. Baxter, CT
Mrs. D. Nelson, NJ
Rabbi M. Richman, PA

Rev. Mr. C. Burton, OH
Mrs. R. Sonen, NJ
Mrs. W. Hydon, NY
Mr. F. Coggan, MI
Calif: Mrs. E. Robert
CT: Mrs. F. Holden
ME,NH,VT: Mrs. C. Broadbent
MA: Mrs. K. Sparrow
NJ: Mrs. G. Fischer
PA: Mrs. D. Parke
NY: Miss S. Steinmetz
Midwest: Mrs. H. Loomis
Outreach: Mrs. W. Tucker

1970-1971:

Pres.: Virginia Lucke, MI
Vice.: Maxine DeBruyn, Zeeland, MI
R.SEC.: Sister Grace, NY
C.SEC.: Winona Cayvan, Grand Rapids, MI
Treas.: Toni Intravaia, IL
Memb.: Wendy Hartman, NY
Prog.: Rev. Daren Miller, NY
Pub.: Marion DuBois, NY
Editor: Judith Bennett, NY
Directors:
Gladys Kanter, MA
Priscilla Baxter, CT
Naomi Aleh-Leaf, MA
Forrest Coggan, MI
Betty Hydon, NY
Pat Sonen, NJ
Alma Nelson, NJ
Rabbi Milton Richman, PA
Rev. Clem Burton, OH
CA: Doug Adams
CT: Betty Holden
MA: Silvia Humphry
Midwest: Ruth Loomis
N. West: Virginia Huffins
NJ: Jean McCurdy
NY: Sally Steinmetz
PA: Avis-Ann Parke
ME,NH,VT: Evelyn Broadbent
Outreach: Alma Tucker

1971-1972:

Pres.: Mrs. Robert DeBruyn, MI
Vice.: Mrs. Irving Kanter, Lexington, MA
R.Sec.: Miss Sarah Parker, N. Y.,NY
C.Sec.: Mrs. Collins Clark, Grand Rapids, MI
Treas.: Mrs. Wm. Muir, Grand Rapids, MI
Memb.: Mrs. Carl Hartman, Pleasant Valley,NY
Prog.: Rev. Daren Miller, Stony Point, NY
Pub.: Mrs. David Parker, Albertson, NY
Editor: Mrs. Lawrence Intravaia, IL
Helps &
Guide.: Mrs. Mal Schlegel, Grand Rapids, MI
Directors:
Forest Coggan, MI
Betty Hydon, NY
Pat Sonen, NJ
Priscilla Baxter, CT
Judith Bennett, NY
Clem Burton, OH
Judy Andersen, MI
Virginia Lucke, MI
Robert Yohn, NY
CA: Doug Adams
CT: Anne Smith
ME,NH,VT: Priscilla Richardson
MA: Jary Yoos
Midwest: Pat Harper
N. West: Virginia Huffine
NJ & PA: Ardyce Thorpe
NY: Sally Steinmetz
Outreach: Alma Tucker

1972-1973:

Pres.: Mrs. Robert DeBruyn, MI
Vice.:
R.Sec.: Miss Sarah Parker, NY
C.Sec.: Mrs. Collins C. Clark, MI
Treas.: Mrs. Wm. W. Muir, MI
Memb.: Mrs. Carl Hartman, NY
Prog.: Mrs. Charles Wolbers, PA
Pub.N.: Mrs. John B. Lucke, MA
Editor: Mrs. Lawrence Intravaia, IL
Helps &
Guides: Mrs. Mal Schlegel, MI

Directors:
Judy Andersen, MI
Virginia Lucke, MI
Robert Yohn, NY
Priscilla Baxter, CT
Judith Bennett, NY
Clement Burton, OH
Forest Coggan, MI
Betty Hydon, NY
Pat Paulsen, NJ

CA: Doug Adams
CT: Anne Smith
E,NH,VT: Priscilla Richardson
MA: Jary Yoos
Midwest: Pat Harper
orthwest: Virginia Huffine
NJ & PA: Ardyce Thorpe
NY: Sally Steinmetz
Outreach: Alma Tucker

1973-1974:

Pres.: Mrs. Robert D. DeBruyn, MI
Vice.: Mrs. Torbin Yates, MA
R.Sec.: Mrs. James Russell, MI
C.Sec.: Mrs. Collins C. Clark, MI
Treas.: Mrs. Wm. W. Muir, MI
Memb.: Mrs. Carl Hartman, NY
Prog.: Mrs. Charles Wolbers, PA
Pub.: Mrs. John B. Lucke, MA
Editor: Mrs. Lawrence J. Intravaia, IL

Directors:
Judy Andersen, MI
Carlynn Reed, CT
Robert Yohn, NY
Forrest Coggan, MI
Mary Bell, IN
Joan Sparrow, MA
Doug Adams, CA
Judy Bennett, NY
Lane Boswell, NY

CA: Jacqueline Meadows
CT: Betsy Reid
ME,NH,VT: Priscilla Richardson
MA: Stanley Arendholz

Midwest: Pat Harper
N. West: Barja Nazaretiz, WA
NJ & PA: Ardyce Thorpe
NY: Sally Steinmetz
Outreach: Alma Tucker

1974-1975:

Pres.: Mrs. Robert D. Debruyn, MI
Vice.: Mrs. Torbin Yates, MA
R.Sec.: Mrs. James Russell, MI
C.Sec.: Mrs. Collins Clark, MI
Treas.: Mrs. Wm. Muir, MI
Memb.: Mrs. Sally Alderdice, NY
Pub. : Mrs. Judith Bennett, NY
Editor: Mrs. Lawrence J. Intravaia, IL
H & G : Mrs. Mal Schlegel, MI
Directors:
Winona Cayvan, MI
Mary Bell, IN
Joan Sparrow, MA
Doug Adams, CA
Margaret Taylor, FL
Lane Boswell, NY
Janet Lee, MI
Carlynn Reed, CT
Robert Yohn, NY
CA: Rev. Jacqueline Meadows
CT: Betsy Reid
ME,NH,VT: Priscilla Richardson
MA: Stanley Arendholz
Midwest: Pat Harper
N.Pac.Cst: Barja Nazaretiz
Northwest: Viginia Huffine
Southeast: Margaret Taylor
Southwest: Susan Bauer
Outreach: Alma Tucker

1975-1976:

Pres.: Mrs. Torbin Yates, MA
Vice.: Rev. Jacqueline Meadows, CA
R.Sec.: Mrs. David Reed, CT
C.Sec.: Mrs. K. A. Sparrow, MA
Treas.: Mrs. Theodore Yoos, MA

Memb.: Mrs. John Alderdice, NY
Prog.: Mrs. Charles Wolbers, PA
Pub. : Mr. Doug Adams, MT
Editor: Mrs. Lawrence Intravaia, IL
H & G: Mrs. Frederic Volz, MA
Directors:
Joan Huff, NY
Margaret Taylor Chaney, FL
Lane Boswell, NY
Janet Lee, MI
Gloria Castano, MA
Robert Yohn, NY
Mary Bell, IN
Maxine DeBruyn, MI
Joan Sparrow, MA
ME,NH,VT: Priscilla Richardson
MA: Stanley Arendholz
CT: Betsy Reid
NJ, PA: Alice Rader
NY: Alice Teirstein
MD,VA,WV,
DC,DE,NC: Dorothy Johnson
S. East: Margaret Taylor
Midwest: Gloria Weyman
MN,ND,SD,
WI: Virginia Huffine
IA,KS,MO,
NE: Marilyn Parks
AR,LA,
OK, TX: Dr. Juana de Laban
CO,ID,MT,
NV,UT,WY: Connie Fisher
AZ, NM: Marjorie Williams
WA: Barja Nazaretiz
OR: Susan Cole
CA, HI: Mary Hynding
I'Natl.: Alma Tucker

1976-1977:

Pres.: Martha Yates, MA
Vice.: Connie Fisher, CO
R.Sec.: Carlynn Reed, CT
C.Sec.: Joanne Sparrow, MA
Treas.: Jary Yoos, MA

Memb.: Sally Alderdice, NY
Prog.: Gloria Castano, MA
Pub. : Douglas Adams, CA
Editor: Toni Intravaia, IL
H & G : Sybil Volz, MA
Directors:
Janet Lee, MI
Evelyn Broadbent, NY
Robert Yohn, NY
Mary Bell, IN
Maxine DeBruyn, MI
Cora Wells, MA
Joan Huff, NY
Margaret Taylor, OH
Jacqueline Meadows, CA
Regional Publicity Directors:
ME,NH,VT: Priscilla Richardson
MA: Stanley Arendholz
CT,RI: Suzanne Valade
NJ,PA: Alice Rader
NY: Carol Vassalo
MD, CA, WV. DC, DE, NC: Dorothy Johnson
AL,FL,GA,MS,SC: Jane C. Mudgett
IL,IN,KY,MI,OH,TN: Faith Clarke
MN,ND,SD,WI: Virginia Huffine
IA,KS,MO,NE: Marilyn Parks
AR,LA,OK,TX: Juana de Laban
CO,ID,MT,NV,UT,WY: Ann Blessin
AZ,NM: Marjorie Williams
WA: Barja Nazaretiz
OR: Susan Cole
CA,HI: Judy Rock
I'Natl: Alma Tucker

1977-1978:

Pres.: Doug Adams, CA
Vice.: Connie Fisher, CO
R.Sec.: Joanne Drouin, NH
C.Sec.: Joanne Sparrow, MA
Treas.: Dorothy Johnson, MD
Memb.: Sally Alderdice, NY
Prog.: Gloria Castano, MA
Pub. : Joan Huff, NY

Editor: Toni Intravaia, IL
H & G : Sybil Volz, MA
Directors:
Mary Bell, IN
Maxine DeBruyn, MI
Cora Wells, MA
Jacqueline Meadows, CA
Robert Yohn, NY
Sylvia Bryant, TN
Judith Rock, CA
Ruth Becker, PA
Ann Blessin, CO
Regional Publicity Directors:
ME,NH,VT: Priscilla Richardson
MA: Dorothy Elliott
CR,RL: Suzanne Valade
NJ, PA: Alice Rader
NY: Evelyn Broadbent
DC,NC,WV,MD,DE,VA: Dorothy Johnson
AL,FL,GA,MS,SC: Jane Mudgett
IL,IN: Mary Bell
OH,KY,MI,TN: Clement Burton
MN,WI,ND,SD: Lois Weeks
NE,IA,MO,KS: Marilyn Parks
TX,LA,AR,OK: Juana de Laban
CO,MT,ID,UT,WY: John Simmons
AZ,NM: Marilyn Onofrio
WA: Norma Rader
OR: Susan Cole
CA,HI,NV: Anne Owens
Canada: Margo Evans
International: Alma Tucker

1978-1979:

Pres.: Doug Adams, CA
Vice.: Carlynn Reed, CT
R.Sec.: Dana Schlegel, PA
C.Sec.: Joanne Sparrow, MA
Treas.: Dorothy Johnson, MA
Memb. : Sally Alderdice, NY
Prog. : Gloria Castano, MA
Pub. : Joan Huff, NY
N.Reg.
Dir. : Alice Rader, PA

Fin.Adv.: Jary Yoos, MA
Editor : Toni Intravaia, IL
H. & G. : Sybil Volz, MA
Directors:
Carla DeSola, NY
Maxine DeBruyn, MI
Connie Fisher, CO
Ruth Becker, PA
Judith Rock, CA
Ann Blessin, CO
Sylvia Bryant, TN
Jacqueline Meadows, CA
Robert Yohn, NY
Regional Publicity Directors:
ME,NH,VT: Priscilla Richardson
MA: Susan Potter
CT,RL: Suzanne Valade
W.PA: Marcia Murray; E.PA: Ruth Anne Rude
NJ: Jerilyn Jefferis
NY: Susan Gunn
DC,NC,WV,MD,DE,VA: Dorothy Johnson
FL,GA,SC: Virginia Shuker
AL,MS: Suanne Ferguson
IL: Babette Payton
IN: Mary Bell
OH,KY,TN: Clement Burton
MI: Kathleen Muir
WI: Ruth Browne
MN,ND,SD: Susan Bauer
NE,IA,KS,MO: Marilyn Parks
TX,LA,AR,OK: Martha Ann Kirk
UT: Cathy Herbut Black
CO,MT,ID,WY: John Simmons
AZ,NM: Marilyn Onofrio
OR,S.W.WA: Susan Cole
WA: Norma Rader
N.CA,NV,HI: Anne Owens
S.CA: Elaine Friedrich
Canada: Margo Evans
International: Alma Tucker

APPENDIX IV

ANNUAL WORKSHOP LEADERS

Feb. 10, 1958

Unitarian Church, Winchester
Miss Barbara Mettler: creative dance an experience for dancer and viewer; all can have creative experience if free; B.M. directed dancers in "interesting and helpful creative dance work."

Feb. 2-3, 1959

Community Church, N.Y.
Robert Storer: "Where do we start?"
Myra Kinch: choreography.
Mary Jane Wolbers: demonstration lesson teaching youngsters; dance in religious education.
The Aviv Dancers: directed by Frances Alenikoff; from Israeli culture.
Louise Mattlage: "Faith Dancing"; her dancers demonstrated.

June 22-26, 1959

(2nd Rel Dance Institute)
Margaret Taylor: rhythmic choir - devotional art more than a dance art -- use whole being, body, mind, & soul; rel. dance does not = modern dance; "religious dance has a strong flowing movement, and a quality of shared ecstasy."
Ted Shawn: choreography; showed his own process in the choreography of "Breath of God".
Jess Meeker: analyzed Bach piece with main motif and variations; groups worked on dance to represent music analysis.
Myra Kinch: workout emphasizing tension and relaxation -- evolved into interpreting "I have sinned, but am forgiven".
Mrs. Backer: taught labanotation.
Evening Program: illustrated theatre dance on religious themes.

Feb. 8-9, 1960

Community Church, N.Y.
Margaret Fisk Taylor
Mary Anthony: outstanding; good knowledge of body and control; creative approach, e.g use of eyes to convey emotion.

June, 1961

Jacob's Pillow
Martha Odom: basic training for beginners.
Jean Fuller: choreographing to poetry; use of props, e.g. material.
Helen Borngesser: organist and director; gave wide choice of music; recommended music with words.
Mary Anthony: need disciplined and controlled bodies; keep dignity in the dance; use facial expression. "If only we presented a body, conditioned and controlled, a temple for the Divine self, when we dance this Divine Being would manifest itself in beauty, truth and power." Don't dance for God, but from God within.
Ted Shawn: gave workout; stressed good strong movement.
Mrs. Rice: on choreography, push self or ego into background in order to release the body for creativity; know your material well.

Feb., 1962

N.Y. Community Church
Donald McKayle: exercises in contraction and extension -- strong movement originates in the torso.
Panel: Walter Sorell, Pauline Koner, Leda Canino; What makes a dance sacred? Practical suggestions: don't mime; let singing or words be prelude to moving to assist audience; experiment with movement; use symbolic props instead of realistic. "In conclusion, sincerity and simplicity with a great deal of self

discipline and technique will accomplish authenticity."

Leda Canino: explored position of standing -- led to improv; used sculpture and mobiles as stimulus.

Evening Vesper: Union Theological Seminary Dance Group.

June, 1962 -- 5th Annual Institute

Craigville Conf. Center, Craigville, Cape Cod

Mary Anthony: technique, choreography; Ecclesiastes "There is a Time".

Jess Meeker: music for dance; played for all classes.

Mary Jane Wolbers: dance from Shakers; congregational response in dance; don't choreograph every word!

Panel Discussion: "Terpsichore and Theology" by guest theologians and dancers.

Feb., 1963

International House, N. Y.

Leda Canino: dancer, choreographer.

Mary Hinkson: dancer, choreographer, Graham Co.

Joseph Canino: artist, lecturer.

Feb. 24-25, 1964

International House, N. Y.

Beverly Hall: dancer, choreographer; taught adults and choir directors for workshop.

Forrest Coggan: dancer, choreographer especially in field of theological themes; taught student technique for workshop.

Barbara Roth: musician for workshop.

Pat Sonen: dancer, writer, creative movement workshops; part of panel.

Rev. Robert Sonen: minister, reader, part of panel.

Rose Lischner: teacher of music, dancer, choreographer, part of panel.

June 26-28, 1964

Drew University, Madison, N.J.
Forrest Coggan: U. of Wisconsin choreographer, author, teacher, advisor to the Guild.
Naomi Aleh-Leaf: choreographer, costume designer; uses variety of Jewish themes.
Barbara Roth: musician, composer.
Worship Resource Committee
Stations of Information: clearing house for specific and individual problems.

Oct. 31, 1964

Crane Theological School of Tufts Univ. Medford, MA.
Diane Pesso: Working with children in Creative movement.
Jeanne Saunders: practical considerations working with motion choirs in the church.

Feb. 22-23, 1965

Universalist Church of New York City
Mary Anthony.

Feb. 25-26, 1966

Interchurch Center & Christ Methodist Church, Riverside Dr., N.Y.
La Meri: choreography, researcher of native dances in many countries;
authority on ethnic dance in world.
Drid Williams: on panel; co-worker with Forrest Coggan; interested in intensity of communication through dance; director of Madison Dance Group.

June 21-23, 1966

Drew University
Naomi Aleh-Leaf: "Dances of the Bible".
Drid Williams: basic positions & meaning in primitive cultures.

Feb. 24-25, 1967

Universalist Church of the Divine Paternity, New York
Pat Birch: dancer, teacher, Graham dancer.
Alan Johnson: dancer, choreographer; specific dance problems; limited space, use of the aisle, steps, platform.
Matteo: concert dancer; use of ethnic dance movement as source for sacred dance.

Feb. 23-24, 1968

Universalist Church of the Divine Paternity, New York
Matteo and Carola Goya: religious expression in ethnic dance; practical look at space problems and lack of floor work.

Feb. 23-24, 1968

Congregational Church Grand Rapids, MI
Harriet Berg: dancer, teacher, "Different Ways of Using the Same Muscles".
Nels Andersen: how to begin a rhythmic choir.
Dr. Lamont Okey: passages from Bible suitable to dance.

June 26-28, 1968

Murray Grove, Lanoka Harbor, NJ
Naomi Aleh-Leaf: "Dances of the Bible and the Near East"; vice-pres. of SDG.; spatial problems.
Art Hall: director of the Afro-American Dance Ensemble, Phil.; technique class.

Feb. 21-22, 1969

1st Un. Methodist Church, Plainfield, NJ
Forrest Coggan: technique.
Ken Thompson: sensitivity training.

June 25-27, 1969

Murray Grove
Ishangi Razak: dirctor, the Ishangi African

Dancers, specializing in African music and dance; exciting technique classes.
Judith Bennett: dancer, choreographer, director of the Wesleyan Dancers; choreography.
Margaret Taylor Chaney: use of contemporary music.

Feb. 20-21, 1970

United Methodist Church, N. Y.
Carol Thaler: Graham student; technique and improvisation.
Linda Rubin: technique and improvisation.

Feb. 20-21, 1970

1st Un. Methodist Ch., Middletown, OH
Toni Intravaia: technique.
Forrest Coggan: "Energy Contours In Life and Art"; idea of relating to point of power located in "far space".

June 23-26, 1970

Murray Grove
Robert Yohn: member of Erick Hawkins Dance Co.; sensitive interpretations, natural movements, different rhythms; dance, religion and life are one.
Charles Creegan: dancer, choreographer, actor.
Daren Miller: theatre, radio, music, dance.

Feb. 19-20, 1971

Summit, NJ
Gladys Kanter
Edward Roll

June 22-25, 1971

Murray Grove
Toni Intravaia: dance director, choreographer, warmups; technique classes.
Clem Burton: organist, choir-master; interpretation of music, poems, choral readings.

<u>Feb. 18-19, 1972</u>

Stony Point Conf. Center, NY
Maxine DeBruyn: Pres. of SDG; technique class.
William Davis, Jr.: dramatic technique and moods.

<u>June 12-14, 1973</u>

Kirkridge, PA
Robert Yohn: dancer, choreographer.
Alice Teirstein: dancer, choreographer; "Biblical Suite".

<u>June 18-21, 1974</u>

Kirkridge, PA
Vija Vetra: East Indian dance.
John Ferguson: music resources.
Maxine DeBruyn, Toni Intravaia, Mary Jane Wolbers: early morning warm-ups and small composition classes.

<u>June 17-20, 1975</u>

Kirkridge, PA
Doug Adams: Congregational Dance and reenacting historic worship with dance.
Mary Craighill: technique and choreography.

<u>June 22-25, 1976</u>

Kirkridge, PA
Gertrude Lippincott: technique and composition.
Gloria Castano: Sessions for Young Students.
Mary Jane Wolbers: Composition.

<u>June 23-26, 1977</u>

Endicott College, Beverly, MA
Moshiko Halevy: Yemenite dances.
Murray McNair: Orff Music
Carole Sivin: Mask making.
Savitri Popkin: Sufi Dance
Rose-Ann Cormier: Yoga.

Doug Adams: Historic Dances in Western Religions and Choreography From Painting.
Mary Ann Hardenbaugh: Thematic ideas.
Robert Yohn: Concepts in performance: "The Empty Pitcher".
Gregory Mitchell: Dance inspired from scripture.
Toni Intravaia: Composition through poetry.
Judy Rock: Dance for the congregation.

June 21-25, 1978

Endicott College, Beverly, MA
Carla DeSola: Dancing the Mass.
Calliope Consort: Music for dance and worship, biblical times to the 17th century.
Hugh Morgan: Body as theatre of the spirit.
Sister Vincent dePaul: Symbolism for movement through visual art.
Doug Adams: Dancing Christmas Carols: Historic and Contemporary.
Carlynn Reed: Truly expressing our relation with God.
Sylvia Bryant: Sacred dance of spirituals and jazz.
Robert Yohn: Themes and variations.
Judith Rock: The choreographer as creator.
Linda Seaton: Scriptual choreography.
Susan Gunn: Technique and choreography.

APPENDIX V

Sacred Dance Guild Membership Statistics:

1958: No Report
1959: No Report
1960: No Report
1961: No Report
1962: No Report
1963: 156
1964: 202
1965: 193
1966: No Report
1967: 233
1968: 262
1969: 262
1970: 252
1971: 222
1972: No Report
1973: 202
1974: 244
1975: 241
1976: 327
1977: 426
1978: 506

APPENDIX VI

Sacred Dance Guild Memb. by State & Country

	1963	1964	1965	1967	1968	1969	1976	1978
AL						1	3	3
AK			1	1	1			
AZ						1	1	1
AR		2	1	1	1	2		
CA	5	7	8	15	18	10	28	91
CO	1	1	1				8	11
CT	25	35	22	15	12	16	13	15
DE		1	1	2	2	1		1
DC					1	1	3	1
FL	1	4	1	1	3	3	4	14
GA					1		2	1
HI			1	1		1	1	
IL	2	2	7	9	8	8	8	16
IN	1	1	1	1	1		3	4
IA	2	2	1	1	2	1	8	6
KS					2	1		1
KY				1	2	1	1	3
LA					1			6
ME	2	2	2	2	3	2		2
MD	1	5	5	4	4	3	5	15
MA	35	31	29	44	41	30	27	25
MI	5	12	15	16	22	36	27	28
MN	2	3	3	4	3	3	2	7
MO								4
MT		1	1	1			3	
NE							3	1
NV								2
NH	9	8	7	5	4	5	13	14
NJ	9	20	13	12	21	23	14	15
NM	1	1	1				2	1
NY	27	30	29	44	46	40	33	35
NC							1	4
OH	4	6	8	11	12	15	21	25
OK		1	4	4	5	4		
OR							6	23
PA	11	9	11	13	17	16	41	59
RI	3	2	1	1	1	1		
SC				1	1			
SD							2	1

	1963	1964	1965	1967	1968	1969	1976	1978
TN				1	2	2	3	5
TX	4	3	3	6	7	8	9	9
UT							1	1
VT	2	4	4	3	4	5		2
VA		1	1	1	4	8	12	8
WA	1	2	4	3	5	5	11	13
WV							4	5
WI	2	2	5	3	4	6	2	6
AUSTRALIA								4
BELGIUM					1			
CANADA	1	4	1	2	2		1	7
ENGLAND								1
JAPAN			1	1				1
SWITZERLAND				1	1	1		

APPENDIX VII

Sacred Dance Degree Programs at Pacific School of Religion, Berkeley, California.

From 1977-1979, the Sacred Dance Guild designated Pacific School of Religion as the recipient of giving by individual members, regional chapters, and national organization giving to establish "The Margaret Taylor Endowment For Dance In Worship and Education" to provide courses to train future ministers and priests in dance. Pacific School of Religion (an interdenominational seminary) was selected in this first three year designation because Doug Adams had been selected to teach worship, preaching, and the arts at the seminary. (where students could therefore emphasize sacred dance at the M.Div. and M.A. level) and to serve on the doctoral faculty in "Theology and Dance" at the Graduate Theological Union in Berkeley (where students could therefore gain Ph.D. programs in Sacred Dance.)
Friends of the seminary provided a $6000 matching challenge grant to stimulate Sacred Dance Guild members from around the country to give to the new Margaret Taylor Dance Endowment. And the new Pacific School of Religion building was designed to provide the largest room with a wooden floor suitable for dance courses, workshops, and performances. Over 400 individuals and groups across the country gave to this successful endowment effort.
The following courses have been offered in Sacred Dance at Pacific School of Religion during 1976-1979 and establish a pattern of curriculum continued at the seminary. Over 300 seminary students have taken sacred dance courses at Pacific School of Religion during this same period. Those interested in pursuing Sacred Dance degree programs leading to the

M.Div., M.A., or Ph.D. should write for details to Doug Adams, Pacific School of Religion, 1798 Scenic Avenue, Berkeley, California 94709. Aiding in the teaching of these courses have been Judith Rock, Karen McClintock, Judith Wagner, Ken Kastler, Robert Yohn, Margaret Taylor, Sandy Park, Barbara Lyon, Anna Halprin, Mary Ann Finch, Carla DeSola, Sylvia Bryant, and Vija Vetra.

RA 151 <u>DANCE TOWARDS WHOLENESS - HEALING</u>
Emphasis will be on movements that allow recreation within self and with others; movements as a means of discovering new perceptions in personal histories and enriched experiences of dance as prayer as well as movement rituals with art, music, and words to develop healing in communities. The movements may be used in education and worship with handicapped people as well as with the handicapped creativity in every person.

RA 152 <u>DANCE IN CONTEMPORARY WORSHIP</u>
The course is designed for beginning dancers as well as those with previous dance experience and those who do not dance but want to know how to incorporate the art of dance in worship settings. There will be regular training in technique and discussion of the basic elements of dance theory and opportunity for practical application exploring various worship settings and different possibilities for dance accompaniment.

SS-RA 177 <u>THE SPIRIT MOVES-DANCE IN WORSHIP AND PRAYER</u>
Danced prayers, exercises for centering, developing ways through movement to illuminate scripture and evoke us to be more involved in the reality and power of the Word. The feasts and seasons of the church year.

RA/FT 191 WORSHIP AND THE ARTS

A team-taught course, using several media to trace the inter-relation of the arts -- dance, music, painting, architecture, speech, and drama -- in shaping Christian worship through history from the modern church to the ancient synagogue. Student input will be chiefly in reading, both from general bibliography and a course anthology.

RA/SS 278 THE SPIRIT MOVES II

The sessions will include danced prayers, exercises for centering and movement techniques, and an experimental group process based on meditation and scripture leading to the choreography of dances expressing the movement of the spirit. Samples from the Omega Liturgical Dance Company repertory will be taught.

RA 302 DANCE IN WESTERN RELIGIONS

The uses of dances in western religions to express the faiths. Experiential sessions and discussion sessions; e.g., Israelite and early church dance and the people's responsibility in history; Eastern Orthodox dance and diversity in community; medieval Catholic dance and problems of authority; Hasidic dance and mysticism; nineteenth century Shaker, frontier camp meeting, Mormon, and black dance and reassertion of equality; and dances in today's religious education, worship and social action.

RA 303 SACRED DANCE IN INDIA

Indian dance is the origin of most dance in eastern religions. The religious significance of Indian dance will be explored through the following: Bharata Natya-Tangore Temple Dancing (dance as worship and story and Nataraja as Lord of the Dance); Manipuri-Assam and Bengal (dance as liturgy); Kathak-North India (dance as rhythm); Kathakali-Kerala (stylistic dance); and Indian Dancing and the relation with Temple art.

RA 304 DANCE IN BLACK RELIGIONS FROM AFRICA TO AMERICA
Forms and meanings of West African dance (studied through film and deYoung Museum collections) serve as background to understand and experience changing dances of Black religions through United States history: "the shout" before and after the 1740 slave code eliminated the drum; nineteenth century dances evolved through contact with white Irish jigs and the camp meeting marching out songs; and twentieth century dances resounding the depths of the spirit from Alvin Ailey's "Revelation" to modern works of the Dance Theatre of Harlem.

RA 305 DANCE IN MODERN WORSHIP AND THEOLOGY
The explosive growth of dance in the 1970's presses the questions explored through movement and discussion: What happens uniquely at the intersection of contemporary dance, worship, and theology? How may dance uniquely illumine theological perceptions and be shaped by those perceptions? What possibilities for embodying the divine-human encounter are suggested by the work of the new generation of avant-garde modern dance choreographers and by the use of dance as hermeneutic of visual arts by modern art museums? An optional modern dance class will be available; also the course will utilize dance films and Bay Area dance performances, both secular and liturgical, for reflection.

RA 307 CRAFT AND CREATION OF DANCE IMAGES
Creating communicative dance with religious dimensions. The class is oriented toward beginners but is open to students at all levels of dance experience as well as students heading toward parish ministry who do not consider themselves dancers but who anticipate encouraging dance in their churches and working creatively with dancers and musicians and congregations. Focus on

elements of dance design, movement dynamics, music and sound for religious dance, problems and possibilities of sanctuary space, relation to congregations, and costume. A twice weekly modern dance technique will be available in conjunction with the class.

APPENDIX VIII: PHOTO HISTORY OF SACRED DANCE GUILD

Margaret Taylor Dancing in 1940s

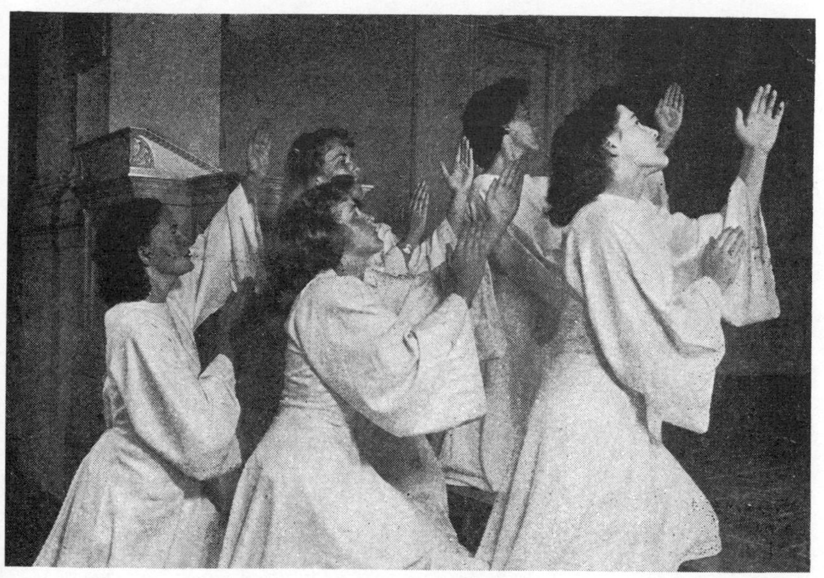

Hanover, New Hampshire 1944 Margaret Taylor
Pilgrim Fellowship Members dancing Bach choral
"Jesu, Joy of Man's Desiring"

"The Dancers of Faith" in "The Demons" directed by Louise Mattlage, 1960

left: Christmas Dance, 1968, International House, Philadelphia, "Dancers of Faith" dir. by Louise Mattlage.

below: Parable of the Wise and Foolish Virgins, United Church of Christ,Philadelphia, 1966, dir.by Mattlage.

below: "Sinfonia Sacra" Lake Edge Congregational Church, Monona Wisconsin, Women at Tomb, 1964, American Mythic Theatre Project, Teatro Internacional Incorporated.

Toni Intravaia and George Allen in "Shough-Nuk-ko-Uck" 1969

Festival Dance MFA Thesis
by Cathy Herbut Black,
Utah, 1972

Holy Week Event, 1973,
Unitarian Dance Fellowship
Madison Wisconsin,
directed by Carol Buse &
Elizabeth Brown

Vija Vetra in Indian Dance and Medieval Western Dance during her frequent Sacred Dance Workshops & Institutes early 1970s

Above: People processing with tripudium step (three steps forward and one back) to "Joy to the World" in worship designed by Doug Adams at Washington National Cathedral, 1975.
Below: Detail of group processing to "Joy to the World"

Terre Sychterz using movement with prayer & song at Reading Pa. St. Catherine of Siena School, 1977.

Dancing out the altar before eucharist at Washington National Cathedral, 1975, dance design by Doug Adams :"Dancing the Eucharist."

Doxology danced by congregation to choreography by Doug Adams at Washington National Cathedral 1975.

Above: "Praise God From Whom All Blessings Flow" (Movement to Doxology during consecration)

Above: "Praise God All Creatures Here Below" (Movement to Doxology during consecration)

left: Paula Douthett, Boulder Colorado Sacred Dance Group at National Cathedral, 1975
right: detail from Murray Spaulding and Sid Miller's dance at National Cathedral, 1975

Above: Connie Fisher leading Congregational Dancing of Doxology, May 1975, Denver Colorado
Below: Helen Gilmore & Hal Taussig mirroring to "Suzanne" in body consciousness through ritual. Philadelphia 1975

Robert Yohn dancing, 1975, at Trinity Church New York "Abraham & Isaac"

Above: Liturgical Dancers under direction of Virginia Blackstock, St. Luke's Chapel, School of Theology, Sewanee, Tennessee, 1976.
Below: "He's Got the Whole World In His Hands" by Halleluiah Dancers, directed by Barbara Leach, 1977 Waterbury Connecticut.

upper photo: Sylvia Bryant dancing, 1977.
lower left: Joan Sparrow dancing Psalm 8.
lower right: Joan Sparrow dancing
"The Masquerader." 1977

Above: Omega Dance Company directed by Carla DeSola, 1977 at Cathedral of St. John the Divine, New York City.

Above: Psalm 27 danced in Presbyterian Church, Temple Texas, choreography by Juana de Laban, 1977

APPENDIX IX
JUNE INSTITUTE
ENDICOTT COLLEGE, MASS.
1977

"Universal Worship Service"

right: <u>Call to Worship</u>:
"When I Consider ...."
Psalm 8 -- Gregory Mitchell

below: <u>Choral Response</u>
"Lift"

This worship service concluded the experiences of the 1977 June Institute.

INVOCATION: "How beautiful upon the mountain ...."
Isaiah 52:7-10 -- Carlynn Reed

left: Prayer "
"You are the one"
Sufi Dance led by
Savitri Popkin

above: Prayer
"Israeli Sabbath"

left: <u>Confession</u> "My Webb"-- Patricia Carhart.

ight: <u>Dance of Affirmation</u> "Tree of Life" -- Judith Rock

left: Martina & Tara Albright, Diana Wolcott
right: Deedee Hardenbergh, Terry Lyn Miller
below: Joan Sparrow, Jary Yoos, Sybille Volz, & Doug Adams

Sermon: "The Man They Say"
-- Robert Yohn & Judith Rock

top: <u>Sermon:</u> "The Man They Say" -- Judith Rock
left: <u>Offering</u>: "Cruciform" -- Robert Yohn
right: <u>Response</u>: "Psalm 100" Make A Joyful Noise --
-- Sylvia Bryant

above:
Benediction
"Chassidic
Dance"

left: Dedication
"Quartet for One
Angel -- Savitri
Popkin

above: Gloria Castano, National Program Director

above & left: Moshiko Halevy, teaching Yemenite dances.

below: Savitri Popkin & Robert Yohn.

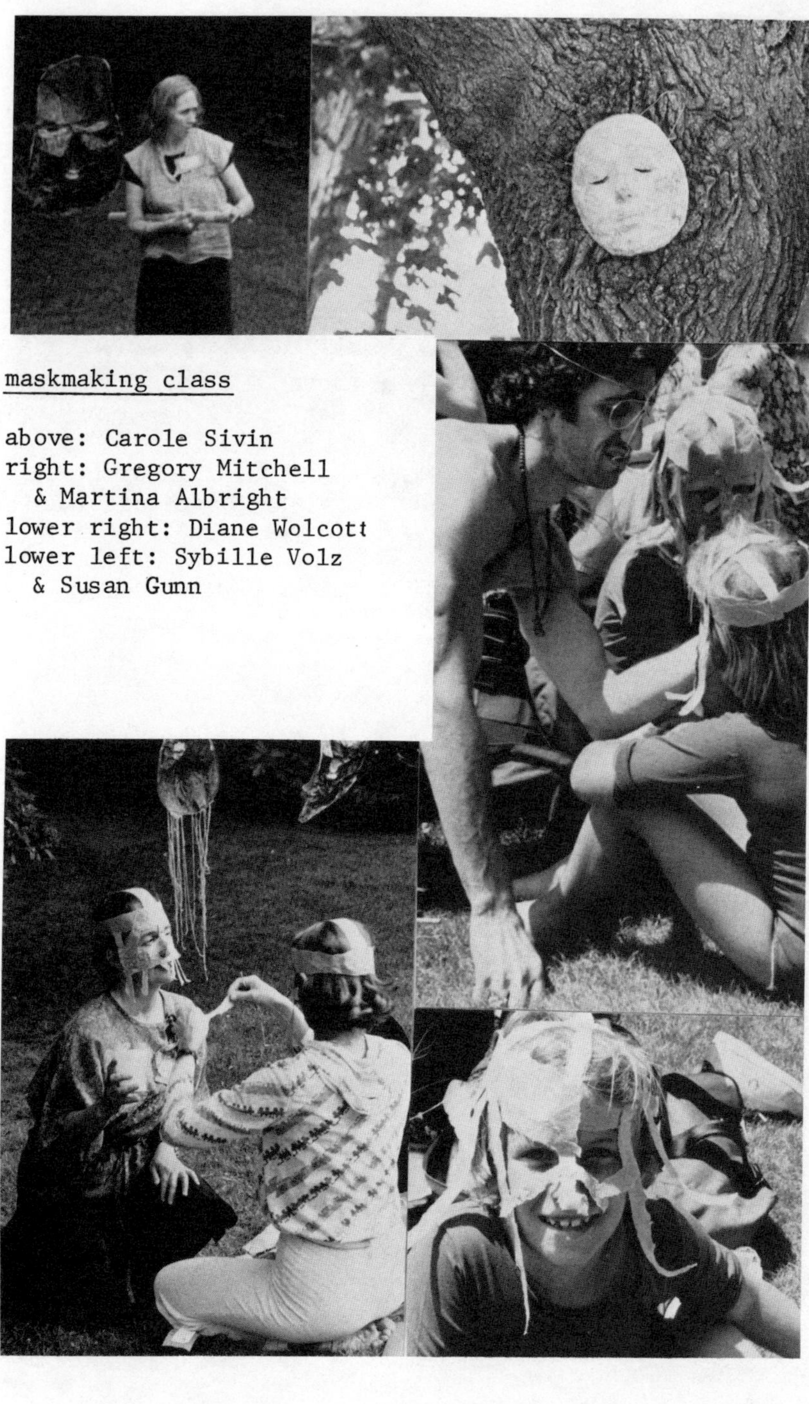

maskmaking class

above: Carole Sivin
right: Gregory Mitchell
& Martina Albright
lower right: Diane Wolcott
lower left: Sybille Volz
& Susan Gunn

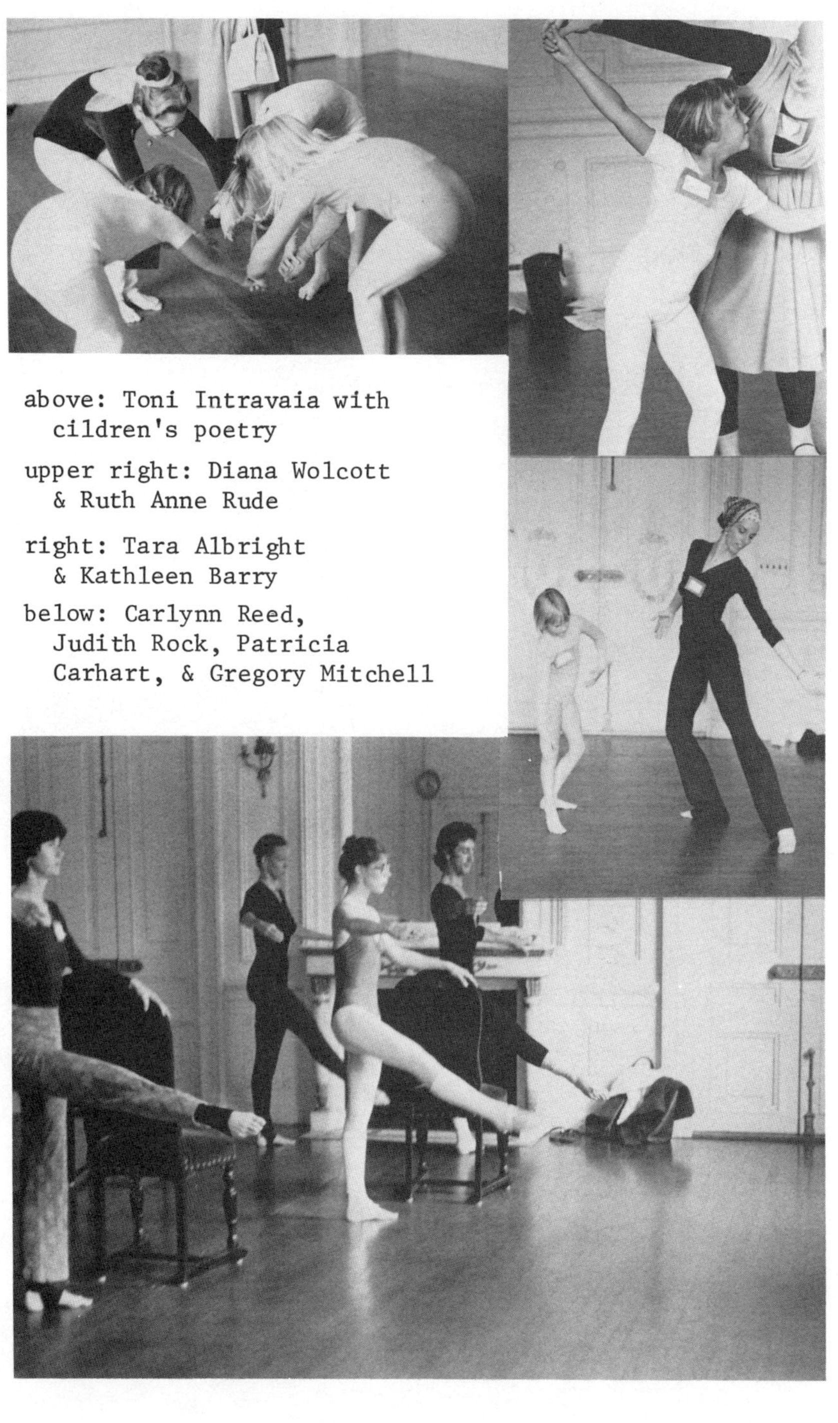

above: Toni Intravaia with cildren's poetry

upper right: Diana Wolcott & Ruth Anne Rude

right: Tara Albright & Kathleen Barry

below: Carlynn Reed, Judith Rock, Patricia Carhart, & Gregory Mitchell

Judith Rock leading the "Dance of Death" at 1977 Sacred Dance Guild Institute in Beverly, Mass.

APPENDIX X: TWENTIETH ANNIVERSARY FESTIVAL
ENDICOTT COLLEGE, BEVERLY, MASS.
JUNE 1978

Above: Festival Leader Carla DeSola instructing group at Notre Dame Chapel, Ipswich,Mass.

Above: Wendy Lee Childs with conference leader Brother Blue and Sister Vincent de Paul SND.

At left: Susan Gunn, modern dance technique class.

below: Brother Blue storytelling through dance-drama.

Reflections on early years of Sacred Dance Guild by Robert Storer (below) and Mary Jane Wolbers (right).

below: Calliope Consort with Sybille Volz (right) leading dance with music & instruments from early church through medieval.

Evening Worship Services:
above: Lutheran worship;
lower left: clown worship;
lower right: interdenominational service with Linda Kahn Seaton signing "Eli-Eli."

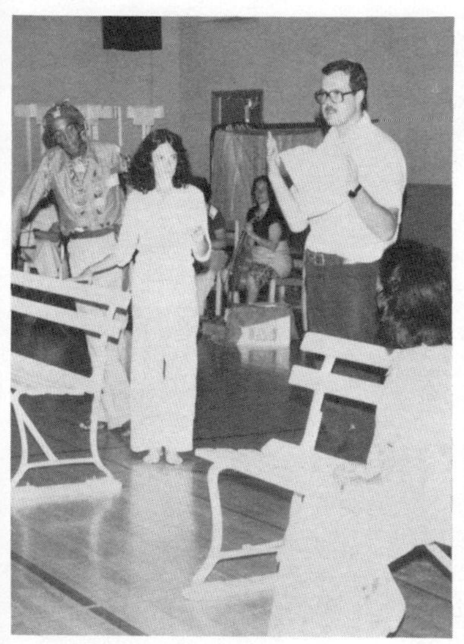

REHEARSING FOR FINAL FESTIVAL WORSHIP SERVICE.
upper left: Father Skip Conlin describes the movement of the Medieval Catholic Mass, as Brother Blue & Carla DeSola listen.
upper right: Lloyd Hobgood & Judith Rock rehearse "Mary Alice's Magnificat." lower middle: Robert Yohn leads group prayer dance.

CLOSING MEDIEVAL MASS WITH DANCE FOR 1978 FESTIVAL CELEBRATED AT NOTRE DAME CHAPEL, IPSWICH, MASS.
upper photo: procession of the dancers
lower photos: entrance of the celebrants

Below: Carla DeSola dancing Mary-Martha.

Below: Judith Rock & Lloyd Hobgood dancing "Mary Alice's Magnificat.

Below: Response In Prayer-Dance at Eucharistic Service.

SELECT BIBLIOGRAPHY

(selected from the recommended reading lists in SDG Newsletters)

Adams, Doug, Congregational Dancing in Christian Worship, (Austin, The Sharing Company, 1976 revised edition), $4.95

____________, Dancing Christmas Carols, (San Jose, Modern Liturgy-Resource Publications, 1978), $5.95 from The Sharing Company.

____________, Involving The People In Dancing Worship: Historic and Contemporary Patterns, (Grand Rapids, The Sacred Dance Guild, 1975), $1.75 from The Sharing Company, P. O. Box 2224, Austin, Texas 78767.

____________, "Bringing The Whole Body To Liturgy," Modern Liturgy, IV,3, (March 1977), This entire issue on Sacred Dance is available through The Sharing Company for $2.50 per copy. (p.2)

____________, "Celebrating Our Diversity and Unity In Liturgical Dance," Modern Liturgy, (March 1977), pp. 4-5.

____________, "The Chagall Jerusalem Windows As Choreography: Stained Glass As Inspiration for Dance In Worship", Stained Glass Quarterly, Vol. 69, No. 2, (Summer 1974), pp. 4-7. $1.25 from The Sharing Company.

____________, "Triumph and Tripudium: A Gesture of Jubilation ...," Modern Liturgy, March 1978), Vol. 5, No. 2, p. 8.

____________, editor of Margaret Taylor's books listed under her name and author of introductions to booklets by Rock and Taussig listed under their names. Also see his columns in the Sacred

Dance Guild Newsletters particularly in 1978 issues for his theological emphasis: e.g. "Moving Sacred Dance from the Axial to the Locomotor" and "Moving Sacred Dance From the Symmetrical to Asymmetrical."

Aker, Suzanne,"To Carol is to Dance," _Dance Magazine_, (December 1964), pp. 40-41.

Andrews, Edward Deming, _The Gift to be Simple_, pp. 3-8, 143-157.

Backman, E. Louis, _Religious Dances in the Christian Church_, The Sharing Co. stocks this book, recently republished by Greenwood Press, New Jersey at $28.00 per copy.

Bennett, Judith, "The Sacred Dance Guild: A Profile," in _Music Ministry_ (Methodist) Feb. 1967.

__________, "Sacred Dance: A Lost Art Reclaimed," in _American Guild of Organists Quarterly_, Apr. 1967.

Black, Barbara Kress, _Barefoot in the Chancel_, Unitarian Press, Boston.

Bruce, Violet R. & Tooke, Joan D., _Lord of the Dance: An Approach to Religious Education_, Pergamon Press, Long Island City, 1966.

Carmines, Al, "In the Congregation of Art," in _Dance Scope_, Fall-Winter 1967-68, pp. 25-31.

Champion, Marge & Zdenek, Marilee, _Catch the New Wind_, Word Book Co., Waco, Texas.

Corita, Sister, _Footnotes and Headlines: A Play-Pray Book_, Herder & Herder, N.Y. 1967.

Cox, Harvey, _Feast of Fools_, Boston, 1969.

Deiss, Lucien & Weyman, Gloria, Dancing for God, World Library of Sacred Music, Cincinnati, Ohio.

__________, Dance for the Lord, World Library Publications, Inc., Cincinnati, Ohio.

Delling, G, "Prayer," in Worship in the New Testament, (London, 1963), pp.104-109.

DeSola, Carla, Learning Through Dance, Paulist Press, N.Y. 1974.

__________, The Spirit Moves: A Handbook of Dance and Prayer, Washington, D.C. Liturgical Press, 1977, $9.95 from The Sharing Company.

__________, & Adams, Doug, "Dancing the Our Father," in Modern Liturgy, March, 1977, Available through The Sharing Company.

Dirksen, Ann, "Introduction to Religious Dance," in Dance Magazine, March 1962.

Fisher, Connie, "Dancing the Old Testament Festivals," in Modern Liturgy, March 1977. Available through The Sharing Company.

Intravaia, Toni, "Motion is a Sacred Thing," in Altar and Home, Conception Abbey, Missouri, July 1960.

Jacques, Odilia Marie, "Dancing as Prayer," in The Lamp, Dec. 1959.

Johnson, Joan S., With Hearts and Hands Uplifted, Bloomington, Minnesota.

Jones, Genevieve, Seeds of Movement, Volkwein Brothers, Pittsburgh, Penn. 1967.

Lowney, Bill, "Continuing Liturgical Dance," in Modern Liturgy, March 1977, Available through The Sharing Company.

Mattlage, Louise, Dances of Faith, The Open Book Store, Fairfield, Conn.

__________, Dances of Faith -- An Affirmation of Life, Exposition Press, Inc., Jericho, N.Y.

Morgenstern, Julian, "The Etymological History of the Three Hebrew Synonyms for 'To Dance'," American Oriental Societal Journal, 36, (1916), pp. 321-332.

Mossi, John, "Celebrational Gestures for Worship Leaders," in Modern Liturgy, March 1977, Available: The Sharing Co.

Oesterley, W.O.E., The Sacred Dance, Dance World Books, 1923.

Ortegel, Sister Adelaide, A Dancing People, 1976.

__________, "Bringing the Whole Liturgy to Dance," in Modern Liturgy, March 1977, Available from The Sharing Company.

Pfautsch, Lloyd, A Day For Dancing, Music Ministry, United Methodist Church, Nashville, Tenn.

Rock, Judith, Theology In The Shape of Dance: Dance In Worship and Theological Process, Austin: Sharing Company, 1978. $2.00

Shawn, Ted, Dance We Must, 1946

Sonen, Pat, Using Movement Creatively in Religious Education, Unitarian Universalist Assoc. Ed. Dept., Boston, Mass.

__________, Sacred Dance: Not for the Eye Alone, Unitarian Universalist Assoc. Press, 1967.

Sorrel, Walter, The Dance Has Many Faces, Columbia University Press.

__________, The Dance Through the Ages, Grosset & Dunlap, 1967.

St. Denis, Ruth, The Divine Dance, Mimeo.

Taussig, Hal, Dancing the New Testament: A Guide to Texts for Movement, The Sharing Company, 1977, Austin, $2.00.

Taylor, Margaret, A Time To Dance: Symbolic Movement To Worship, Austin: The Sharing Company, 1976 revised edition, $5.95

__________, Dramatic Dance With Children in Education and Worship, Austin: The Sharing Company, 1977, $7.95.

__________, Creative Movement: Steps Toward Understanding, New York: Friendship Press, 1969, $1.50 from Sharing Co.

__________, Look Up and Live: Dance As Prayer, Austin: The Sharing Company, 1977 $4.95.

__________, Considerations For Starting and Stretching A Sacred Dance Choir, Austin: The Sharing Company, 1978, $2.75.

Margaret Fisk Taylor Chaney's books are available through The Sharing Company, P. O. Box 2224, Austin, Texas 78767.

Terry, Walter, Ted Shawn, Father of American Dance, The Dial Press, N.Y. 1976.

Troxell, Kay, "Dance for Lent: The Lamb of God," in Modern Liturgy, March 1977, Available: The Sharing Co.

Weyman, Gloria, "Understanding: The Key to Approval," in Modern Liturgy, March 1977, Available: The Sharing Co.

Wosien, Marie-Gabrielle, Sacred Dance: Encounter With the Gods, The Hearst Corp., N.Y. 1974.

Yates, Martha, "The Sacred Dance Guild," in Modern Liturgy, March 1977, Available: The Sharing Co.